Building a Firm Foundation

Medina County Architecture
1811-1900

Published in 1995 by
McKiernan/King
233 South Court
Medina, Ohio 44256

All rights reserved. For permission to reproduce
information or images from this book, contact
the publishers.

Library of Congress Catalog Card Number 95-94896
ISBN 0-9648275-0-6

Research and text by Susan Paolano McKiernan and
Joann Garwood King.

Design and layout by Susan Paolano McKiernan and
Sean Mathias McKiernan.

Cover photograph by Kevin Olds.
Printed by Austin Printing, Akron, Ohio.

Building a Firm Foundation

Medina County Architecture 1811-1900

Susan Paolano McKiernan   Joann Garwood King

Graphic production by Sean Mathias McKiernan

Contents

Preface	5
Medina County History	7
Log Structures	10
New England Farmhouse	14
The Federal Style	15
The Saltbox House	21
Greek Revival	23
York Township "Greeks"	33
Valley City "Greeks"	35
Western Reserve	37
Monitors	40
Schools	41
Gothic Revival	47
Churches	49
Cemeteries	57
The Victorian Era	60
"Gingerbread"	62
The Italianate Style	63
Second Empire	68
Public Buildings	70
George Gruninger	76
Lanterns	77
Stick Style	80
Eastlake	84
Queen Anne	88
Lost Towns, Forgotten Places	91
Shingle Style	93
People	100
Vernacular Architecture	102
The Farmhouse	106
Barns	110
Roads and Bridges	117
Commercial Buildings	119
Classical Revival	141
National Register Properties	144
Glossary	145
Acknowledgements	148
Photo Credits	148
Bibliography	151
Index	154

Preface

Our project began with a simple objective: to survey Medina County's architecture. However, the scope of the task became clear only when we began to document Medina County's historic sites and buildings and relate them to the people and events from the time of the first permanent settlement in 1811 to the turn of the twentieth century.

Fortunately, early maps in the 1874 and 1897 Medina County atlases provided valuable information. Each township and village map has small symbols indicating houses, schools, churches, and cemeteries. We plotted these properties on current township maps which acted as our travel guides. Armed with these resources and the Ohio Historic Inventory survey conducted by the county in 1979, we covered every road that existed prior to 1900.

Initially, our criterion for noting a property was unstructured. We did not want to confine our survey only to domestic architecture, but rather to consider any structure that would tell us something about building practices in the county. This included homes, commercial and public buildings, churches, schools, barns and other outbuildings, fences and stonework. Architecturally significant structures and details, all dated barns, and all sixty-one cemeteries and burial plots were also documented. We located and photographed buildings pictured in the early atlases even though their appearance had measurably changed. Abandoned and derelict buildings were included so that there would be some record of their existence. Over 1500 examples were collected for reference.

The next objective was to sort the photos by township and architectural period and pare them down to a manageable number for a book. This was a difficult task because so few of the many excellent examples could be included. Also, it was important to us to represent each township. We used existing photographs whenever possible in order to offer a view of a property in an early setting and condition. Other sites were photographed by Pat Bishop, a faculty member at The University of Akron well known for her work. Photographers Andrew Borowiec, Kevin Olds, and Al Teufen also contributed images, as did Cleveland artist Don Harvey. Once the properties were selected, the research began, linking the buildings to those who built and occupied them. It was, after all, the people of Medina County who made the style choices and shaped the county as we see it today. Again the early maps served as excellent tools, as they provided landowners' names and township lot numbers. With this information we were able to track the properties in the county land records to find the subsequent owners. We then traced the names through the county tax duplicates from 1826 (the earliest available) to 1900 to determine construction dates. In some cases, property owners or local residents were able to contribute valuable information as well.

To understand the motives of the people, we read all the Medina County *Gazettes* from the 1870s to 1900, looking for specific references to any building; i. e., barn raisings, housing construction, painting and improvements, building moves—anything that indicated

Federal buildings on the west side of Medina square before the fire of 1870.

what was being built and how. While we read, we garnered information about leading citizens, special events, economic conditions and style trends. Local histories, diaries, conversations, letters and obituaries filled more blanks.

So what did we find? We discovered that Medina County has a rich heritage of architecture from the early log cabin to the Classical Revivals at the turn of the century. We found that even though Medina County has had a recent period of enormous growth and development, there is still a strong representation of early architecture throughout the county. And finally, we learned that the county has a marvelous diversity within its borders: regional styles and building techniques that seem to be significant just for a small area. This includes brick Greek Revival homes and red slate roofs in the northwest, square silos in the northeast and central sections, and large farmsteads at the end of extended lanes in the southeastern townships.

The final task, of course, was to gather all this information into an understandable whole. This book is the result. It is our hope that the reader will become more familiar with Medina County's architectural environment and appreciate even more its rich heritage. Those who came before us built with style and skill. What remains says a great deal about their traditions, current conditions, and future ambitions. They applied their inherited values to their architecture and in doing so, they built a firm foundation for us.

The south side of the square in ashes after the fire of April 15, 1870. Although no lives were lost, forty buildings burned, and the Courthouse caught fire six times before the fire burned itself out. The stepped gable Federal Phoenix building was totally destroyed but its safe was dragged to the street to safety.

The west side of Medina square as rebuilt in the Italianate style after the 1870 fire.

Medina County History

Long before the first pioneer ventured into the Ohio country, Native Americans used this area for hunting, traveling by canoe or walking the trails and ridges. As early as the Paleo period, man built shelters, gathered food and hunted animals that have long been extinct. There is evidence here, in the form of charred postholes, of lodges or shelters that date to 10,000 B.C.

The Chippewa, Wyandotte, Delaware and Ottawa peoples left their mark on the land now known as Medina County. Chippewa Lake, named after the nation that frequented its shores, is evidence of their presence. Arrowheads and tools still surface in the spring plowing. Many of the county's roads were originally trails. Smith Road was part of the Watershed Trail, the major east-west route from Pittsburgh to the West. State Route 224 was an early trail, as well. At one time there were mounds and earthen forts. Many have been leveled by continuous farming and development, but Mound Hill Cemetery in Seville stands as testament to Native American engineering.

These eighteenth-century woodsmen built substantial, though temporary, buildings. They were constructed of available materials by securing bent saplings to the ground. A covering of hides and bark served as the walls and roof. As there were no permanent settlements in Medina County, these houses served only as temporary shelter during hunting season. When the families returned to their villages along Lake Erie, the lodges were dismantled for transport or left for the next season. Early settlers left written descriptions of these structures.

In 1662, Charles II of England chartered to the Colony of Connecticut all lands from Connecticut to the Pacific Ocean, between the 41st and 42nd parallels, excepting New York and Pennsylvania. In 1787, the new Federal government passed the Northwest Ordinance establishing the Northwest Territory and made provisions for its organization and settlement. The new government wanted to claim these state-owned reserves and sell the land to repay its Revolutionary War debts. By 1794, the State of Connecticut settled its claim for land in the Northwest Territory but reserved the northeast portion as the Connecticut Western Reserve. In 1796 the state sold this land to the Connecticut Land Company which surveyed it, paving the way for settlement. The Native Americans were pushed further west, except for small family groups who chose to live among the pioneers.

In 1807, the Connecticut Land Company held a lottery for lands in New Connecticut and each investor drew lots according to the amount invested. Elijah Boardman of Milford, Connecticut invested $60,000 and drew the areas of Medina Township and Boardman Township on the eastern edge of the Reserve. After the land was

allotted and surveyed, the first settlers arrived in Harrisville and Liverpool Townships in 1811.

This land, canopied with unbroken forest, was not totally secure for settlement until after America's victory in the War of 1812. Many who did come in 1811 left temporarily until the British were defeated and the threat of uprisings removed. In 1812, the Ohio State Legislature formed Medina County, but attached it to Portage County until 1818 when there were enough people in the area to form their own government. Elijah Boardman made certain that the county seat rested on his property by donating the land for county buildings and a public square.

There was no distinct pattern to Medina County's growth. Each township had different owners who provided for the survey and sent out a land agent to represent them. Joseph Harris arrived in Harrisville Township as a land agent and Justus Warner came to Liverpool in 1811. In Litchfield, Judge Holmes, the original investor, arrived in 1812 and cleared one acre of land. Further settlement was delayed when he ran into financial trouble and put his land back on the market. In 1814, the first parties came to Medina and Wadsworth townships. Brunswick was settled in 1815, Sharon in 1816, and Guilford and Westfield in 1817. Both Montville and Chatham opened for settlement in 1818. The owner of Granger Township sold the first parcel in 1820, but kept the western part, Remsen Tract, a dense forest until the 1840s. The first settler in Spencer arrived in 1823. Samuel Hinckley was slow to develop his land because he had more valuable land elsewhere. Hinckley was not organized until 1825. Lafayette and York were organized in 1830 and finally, Homer Township in 1831.

When Medina County was first platted in 1818, it also contained Norton, Copley, Bath, Richfield, Grafton, Sullivan, Penfield and Huntington Townships. Later, the western townships were combined into Lorain County, and the four eastern townships became part of Summit County. By 1839, the county as we know it today was organized, leaving Medina with its familiar stair-step border.

Since Easterners purchased most of the land, many of the early settlers were from the New England states, particularly from Connecticut. By the 1840s, there was a strong contingent of Germans from both Pennsylvania and the "old country" that settled in the western and southern portions of the county. Subsequent architecture shows the influence of these distinct groups.

The way was not easy for these early settlers. They came in the fall with enough food to get through the winter, along with an ax to fell the trees, a blanket for warmth, and a bell to locate wandering oxen. By the spring they had built a rude cabin and cleared an acre or two for the first crop. They often returned to their native homes to collect their families or find a wife to share life on the frontier. The wealthy family settling on speculation, arriving with good china, family heirlooms, and silk clothing lived for a few years in the same type of crude log house as the lone settler arriving with all of his belongings in his pack. Today's county map reflects their endeavors—Nettleton, Foskett, Fenn, and Simcox roads are named after the families that opened them.

Often the first wave of pioneers came in family groups and migrated west with others from their Eastern villages. Settlers who followed benefited from the ready help and advice from those who had learned how to fell the trees, raise cabins, and clear the woods. Early accounts tell of the woods ringing with the sound of axes on wood and the air filled with smoke from the vast fires. Pioneer women tended the fires while their husbands chopped wood into the night. Indigenous oak, walnut, tulip, ash, and maple logs five feet wide were burned and the ashes carried east to be made into charcoal for the iron foundries.

Clara Reyser and her family on their Homer Township porch.

By the advent of the Civil War, Medina County was fully settled. It's economy was primarily agricultural with an emphasis on dairying and woolgathering. Transportation was still by horse and buggy or very slow stage coach. In 1818, the Wooster Pike opened from Medina to Seville and in 1820, it was made a state road extending south to Wooster and north to Cleveland. The Pike was the main "course" with stage coach stops in Seville, Medina and Brunswick. Another stage line carried mail and passengers to Akron on the road now known as Route 18.

Even though the citizens were somewhat isolated, they still were concerned with the major contemporary issues. The right to vote was taken seriously and political debates were fervent. Literary societies and libraries sprang up in each village. Prohibition groups developed in response to the severe alcohol problem. There are at least nineteen documented Underground Railroad stations in Medina County. Medina's young men fought with the "Bloody Eighth" at Antietam and marched with Sherman to the sea. The county's cemeteries are filled with markers and monuments that commemorate their sacrifice.

After the War, Medina entered the Industrial Era. Wadsworth completed the first rail line in 1863, opening markets for that township's coal. In 1871 the Lake Shore Railroad and in 1890 the Northern Ohio line created new markets for the county's goods, produce, and natural resources. Prosperity came hand-in-hand with new industry and easy access to markets.

There were setbacks to this progress. In 1848, and again in 1870, most of Medina town square burned. After the 1870 fire, the townspeople rallied and rebuilt in brick in the Victorian styles that give the city its distinctive flavor.

Throughout the last decades of the nineteenth century, the county grew and prospered. Tobacco grew in Westfield and Guilford Townships and several communities had cigar factories. Celery and other produce flourished in the muck land near Lodi. Wadsworth was a major coal-producing area in the 1870s and 80s. Ohio Match, Ohio Injector, and Ohio Salt were large Wadsworth industries at the end of the century. A.I. Root and the Hollow Ware Foundry (later Henry Furnace) were important Medina companies. At Chippewa Lake, Ed Andrews opened one of the country's first leisure resorts which remained popular for over a century.

From the first log shelter with its earthen floor and meager existence, Medina County grew to a community of industry and agriculture. Its diverse architecture encompasses many styles, from the primitive homes of the early settlers to the fussy styles of the Victorians. Each township grew in response to its own resources and needs. Styles varied by area based upon the ethnic make-up of the community and building traditions and skills. The history and development of the county can be chronicled through its architecture from the first rustic cabin to the complex Victorian styles at the turn of the century.

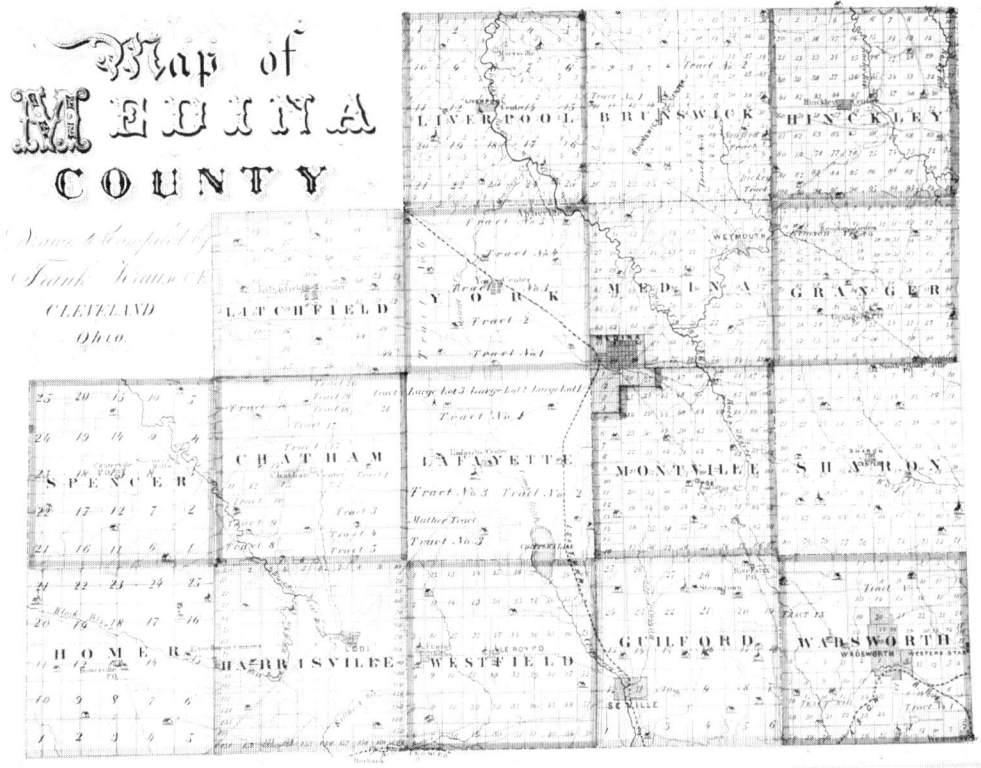

Log Structures

The settlers came from New England with a long tradition of timber-frame construction, but two factors forced them to build log cabins in the style of the Swedes and Germans. First, their only tool was the ax; they had no saw or plane with which to make boards. Second, the land was covered with trees which had to be removed before they could plant crops for their survival. With a single tool and a few neighbors (in the early days, eight or ten miles was not too far to walk to help a "neighbor" raise a cabin), a pioneer could clear a spot of land and erect a home at the same time. Many more trees would be used to heat the inhabitants and cook their food over the next decade or so until a "proper" house was built.

By 1812, the land now known as Medina County was open for settlement. The threat of war was over, and Eastern investors were anxious to profit from their holdings in the Western Reserve. The pioneers came west looking for cheap, rich farmland. But when they arrived, they found giant walnut, maple, oak, and poplar blanketing the area. According to one writer, the forest was so dense that a squirrel could go from Cincinnati to Cleveland without touching the ground.

For the settler, this abundance was a formidable enemy—the first obstacle to civilization. The woods sheltered preying animals that killed livestock. It blocked out sunlight and restricted cultivation of crops. The first objective was to make a "cut" or clearing which would become the nucleus for a thriving farm. In that clearing the Medina settler raised his first home. Taking advantage of available natural materials and a tradition of frame building, he built his home of wood.

There is a distinction between log cabins and log houses. N.B. Northrop writes in *Pioneer History of Medina* about Henry Hosmer's "hewed log house, two stories high, considered a model edifice, and contrasting wonderfully with... the first cabins that had been built". A cabin was a primitive, temporary shelter made of bark-covered logs chinked with moss or mud. Smoke escaped through a hole (a "windeye") in the roof or a chimney made of sticks. A log house, however, was made of hand-hewn logs and chinked with wedges of wood or stones and plaster. It had a shingled roof and there were windows of oiled paper or small panes of glass brought from the East. Log buildings were often covered with clapboards, particularly after the sawmills were in operation, and many of them survive as outbuildings or as rear sections of later houses.

When David and John Wilson first arrived on their land at Wilson's Corners, later called River Styx, they built a temporary shelter of basswood logs only six by ten feet in area. Their beds were poles wedged between the logs and covered with bear skins. Their pillows were "the fat part of an arm". In 1816, the Hinsdales came to Wadsworth and built a similar structure, but they waited until winter to chink it in order to allow the logs to shrink. Albert Hinsdale said that his home looked like a pierced tin lantern when approached at night.

Although one man could erect a rough, temporary cabin, the construction of a decent log cabin or house took many hands. Community members gathered to assist one another, and this interdependence afforded an opportunity for socializing. In Guilford Township, John Coolman assured ample help by promising a gallon of whiskey to the first team to arrive on the scene. Henry Hosmer and company arrived at 2:00 am, took a good drink, and slept until the others arrived. In 1820, Wadsworth's Congregational church was raised without benefit of whiskey, "something that had never been tried before". Rufus Ferris had a barn raising in Medina and provided two pails of milk punch. After a full day of work and drink, some were on their backs "feeling upward for terra firma".

The raisings were generally orderly affairs, however. The most experienced man served as captain. He selected the best axmen who cleared the site and cut the logs into suitable lengths. Others chose a large, straight-grained oak and split it for roof clapboards. Lengths of chestnut, oak, or ash were dressed with an adz for a puncheon floor and door and window casings. Expert corner men notched the logs and stripped them of their bark to deter insects. The corners carried the weight of the house, so careful notching was imperative. Slowly, the four walls went up as the stronger men pushed the logs up a make-shift tramway, using forked poles. Gable logs, roof ribs, and a ridge pole finished the job. They then covered the roof with clapboards, hinged the door, and set the tiny windows. If the landowner already had the logs cut and placed for raising, the house could be built in a day.

The pioneer woman's primary roll was to prepare and serve the food. When her house was finished, she planted a red cedar by the front door in celebration. Years after many of the original log houses disappeared, a lone cedar marked the spot of that first raising.

When the settler had built his simple shelter, he turned his energy toward clearing more land and developing a farm. First the smaller trees and brush were cleared and burned. Then a girdle of notches was cut into the bark of the large specimens. As the trees slowly died, corn and potatoes were planted around the huge trunks. The next year the tree gave up its large branches and the trunk was left to rot or burned in place. Now the open field was ready for wheat. In this manner, the forests gave way to fields, acre by acre. It is difficult to imagine that trees were considered a burden. A visitor from England lamented the felling of whole forests and noted that many of the trees were fifty feet tall to the first branch! By the end of the nineteenth century, Medina County was stripped of its virgin timber. Trim farmhouses replaced log ones and Victorian-era photographs show homes standing in open terrain, barren of trees except for the orchard and symbolic cedar.

Log houses continued to be built to the end of the century in Spencer and Homer Townships, isolated communities with strong German traditions. There is a vast difference, however, between early and late log houses. Store-bought nails, glass, lamps, and carpets offered comforts and conveniences that the pioneers longed for. A log cabin built in 1830 in York Township had a store-bought stove which the neighbors admired with curiosity. The Homer Township cabin illustrated has wallpaper glued directly onto the logs.

Some mourned the passing of the log houses as they gave way to more refined forms of architecture. But for many who had lived in them, the memories were less than romantic. With only a fireplace for heat, pioneers remembered being "half frozen". To keep warm, families retired for the night at 8:00, all in one bed. As neighboring pioneers cleared their land, acrid smoke from the burning fires blocked out the sun. Yet these simple cabins have been romanticized more than any other type of American home, and many politicians pretended to trace their roots to boyhoods in log houses in the woods. Even today this humble building is synonymous with hearth and home.

On April 10, 1817, a small band of Episcopalians and Congregationalists gathered in Medina Township to build the first house of worship. They met at dawn, felled and notched the trees, and held services by 4:00 pm. Because the cabin was meant only as temporary shelter, the beams were neither hewn nor chinked. The roof was made of rough shingles held in place with poles, and the door and windows were hides. Despite its simplicity and small size, the primitive cabin served as a church for both congregations and as the local school and meeting house.

Abraham Hard II was born in New Milford, Connecticut in 1766 and moved with his family to Vermont as a young boy. At the age of twenty-three he married Rebecca Flagg of Shrewsbury, Massachusetts, and they had ten children together. Abraham and Rebecca came to Wadsworth Township in 1818 and built this house soon after they arrived. Its logs are beech, walnut, oak and maple. The house survives today because it was covered with clapboards and continued to be used as a home for many years. Like other early log buildings, the Hard house was used as a meeting house (in this case, for a society of Methodists) as well as a home for "Father" Hard, his wife, and five of their nine children. Mr. Hard died in 1844. Mrs. Hard died in 1860 in her ninety-second year, leaving five generations of Hard Family descendants.

Rudulphus Schniebly built his log house in Homer Township about 1845. Homer and Spencer Townships were largely settled by Pennsylvania Germans who had a tradition of log building. These townships were not settled until the 1830s, and the first sawmill was not built until 1835, so that log buildings continued to be erected much later in these areas. When first constructed, this log house had a taxable value of $46.

The relocation of this Harrisville Township log house in 1872 prevents specific dating, although it was probably built in the 1830s. The carefully dressed corners and level, even walls (all hewn with only an ax) indicate that it was meant to be sided immediately upon construction. Several additions enlarged the house over the years, but a tornado destroyed all but the most solid part, the original log section. The Medina County Historical Society acquired this house in 1994 and has dismantled it for future reconstruction.

New England Farmhouse

The Colonial farmhouse or "New England Large" domestic style developed over the first two centuries of New England's settlement. It is a vernacular Georgian house: a rectangle with symmetrically spaced and sized windows, and an austere facade except for the central door. These houses were popular in New England from about 1750 to 1790. Most of the early settlers in Medina County were from Connecticut, followed by New York and Vermont. In 1870, John Brongers claimed that the population of Hinckley was made up entirely of Connecticut Yankees except for three families from England. Consequently, the settlers built in familiar styles, and Medina County resembled the Connecticut landscape in the first half of the nineteenth century.

E.A. Warner was born in Connecticut in 1799 and came to Medina County in 1817. He built a log cabin for his father, James, and family on the center lot of Medina Township. The Warners lived in the log house while settling their farm.

James Warner purchased the Bagdad sawmill in 1819 and built this house in 1826. Its taxable value was $420, a high price which indicates its considerable quality and size. It is a New England Colonial house built long after such houses were popular in New England.

Warner either built in the style he was familiar with, or wanted what he thought of as a "proper" house to signify his position. It has a massive center chimney, since stoves were not available in the county until about 1830. The central position for the chimney allows fireplace openings into several rooms and dissipates heat throughout the house.

The virgin hardwood clapboards were not painted, but weathered to a warm grey over the years. During this time, houses were so rarely painted on the frontier that an "Indian red" house in Cleveland was worthy of mention in contemporary accounts. The shallow gable roof, originally wood shingled, follows the New England tradition and allows taller ceilings in the second-story rooms. Chestnut shingles were split from local woods or cedar ones were imported from the huge cedar bogs near Springfield, Ohio.

The windows are large, but the sashes are made of tiny panes of glass (twelve-over-twelve). Glass still had to be hand made and imported from Pittsburgh or Zanesville and was one of the most expensive materials in the house. The windows are of equal size and symmetrical placement, and the door is in the exact center. The house is quite plain except for a segmented ribbon or transom window over the door, an element held over from the Georgian Period. What an impression Warner house must have made—a manor house transplanted from an English estate to the Ohio wilderness!

The Federal Style

The impact of the Federal house on the Medina countryside in the 1820s and 1830s cannot be overemphasized. While there were many Greek Revival houses by the end of the 1830s, the most common house was still a log cabin. Imagine a two story house with towering chimneys, symmetrically-placed doors and glass windows, regular, ordered room placement, and hewn stone lintels standing out among rough cabins with haphazard windows and one or two tiny rooms. Compare polished wooden floors with tamped earth ones and painted plaster walls to bare logs, well-lit, spacious rooms to low, gloomy ones, and, most importantly, the privacy of individual rooms to a single room and a loft for all the family's activities.

The Federal style of architecture was influenced by the English architects and designers Robert and James Adam. It was popular in the East about 1790 to 1820, when the forests of Medina County were yet to be tamed and log cabins were the rule. The population of Medina county grew seven times between 1820 and 1850, but the majority of settlers came with very little. By 1820, Medina Village had only one "decent, finished" house. York Township had only three frame houses by 1839.

For the wealthy settlers who wanted to duplicate the civil, urban architecture of their hometowns in the East, the Federal was the chosen style, particularly after sawmills made milled lumber available. In some cases, the builder with access to clay and mortar fired bricks for construction. Although nails were made in Cleveland in 1816, the fact that iron foundries were rare and nails were made by hand made them very expensive. When Julia Loomis died in Wadsworth in 1820, Jacob Miller could find only eighteen nails to make her coffin. Phineas Butler pulled fourteen more from the house he was building so that she could have a casket. He had brought the nails with him from New York.

The Federal is a feminine, graceful style with elegant proportions and delicate detailing. There is little surface decoration. The beauty of the Federal design comes from its elegant, ordered placement of door and window openings and the delicacy of its proportions. The positioning and size of the windows, the amount of unadorned wall space, the shallow roof, the understated decoration of the doorway, and the lack of a porch to break the unified surface create a style which has never been out of fashion in America. White and pastel colors such as buff, stone, and pale yellow add to the delicate, feminine quality.

One type of Federal building places the gable end to the street. This type is common in Eastern towns with narrow lots, taxed upon their width. These gable-front Federals were also built on the frontier by people familiar with this type, or who expected their neighborhood to grow into a town and be taxed accordingly. For others, building in an established style showed their Eastern civility and urbanity.

The other type of Federal house, more common in Medina County, has the long end as the facade. Divided into five bays, it has a center door topped by a window and flanked by two symmetrical rows of windows. Chimneys top both end walls. The facade is quite simple except for the doorway, which is often recessed or trimmed with thin, fluted columns, Ionic capitals, or a fanlight, depending upon the skill of the builder and the taste and finances of the owner. Carpenters and joiners on the frontier used skills, methods, and tools known to their ancestors. The drill, adz, saw, ax, maul, froe, wedge, plane, and gouge had been in use since Medieval times and were not supplanted until the Industrial Revolution.

Russell Burr, Jr. and his brother George arrived in the area now known as Lodi in February of 1811. There were no other settlements in Medina County. The nearest neighbors were in Wooster, seventeen miles south without a road cut to it, and Randolph, twenty-five miles east, connected by a trail of blazed trees. It is difficult to comprehend the frightening isolation of these early settlers.

Burr erected the first frame building in Harrisville Township, a thirty by forty foot barn, in 1816. In the late 1820s he built this wonderful temple-front Federal house. The name of the designer/carpenter is beyond discovery, but the house stands as the finest example of Federal surface adornment in the county. The doorway has fluted columns, dentil molding, and Ionic capitals, all hand carved. They are elements of the Federal style, Classical motifs selected for their light, delicate quality. The egg-and-dart molding and shell are particularly beautiful.

Western Star was one of the county's earliest settlements, dating from 1814. This Federal style house was built by Jacob Miller, one of Wadsworth earliest settlers, in 1830. Miller was known to have been a carpenter and may have built this house for himself. According to *Wadsworth: Center to City*, clay for the bricks was dug nearby and mixed with water by driving oxen through it. The house was stuccoed and made into apartments in the 1930s, but the twelve-over-twelve sash windows are original.

Barney Spooner built "the Castle on the Hill" in Marysville, Liverpool Township. The 1835 brick Federal has nine fireplaces and a beehive oven in the basement. The four flanking chimneys which form the top of the stepped gable are a notable characteristic of one type of Federal building, as is the semi-circular arch over the door.

Rufus Ferris, a land agent for Elijah Boardman from New Milford, Connecticut, arrived in Medina in 1816. He built a double-pen log cabin for his first home which served as a church and meeting place and temporarily housed many settlers upon their arrival in the area. He erected the first frame barn in the village in 1817 with help of "neighbors" from Liverpool and Brunswick. He built this house, the first brick house in the village, in 1825. The hip roof and deep profile are rare in the Federal style, but the Ferris house has the familiar five bay facade, flanking chimneys and symmetry. This photograph was taken in 1952.

Calvin Jarvis' house in Seville has many of the hallmarks of the Federal style: delicate proportions, a shallow roofline, balanced symmetry, an emphasized doorway, flanking chimneys, and a lunette or fanlight window over the door. It was built before 1830.

This house, listed on the National Register of Historic Places, was built for George Burr, a prominent Lodi settler, before 1830. The three-bay brick arcade is rare in northeastern Ohio, but the flanking chimneys and fanlight window over the door are typical elements of the Federal style. The Burr house was Victorianized with gingerbread trim in the 1880s.

Federal architecture often makes use of a semi-circular or ovoid element. This small-paned window with a lunette or fanlight is influenced by the work of the Classical Italian architect Palladio. The window's carved wooden columns, Doric capitals, arch, and keystone add vitality to this otherwise unadorned house/coaching inn built in the 1820s in Seville. As was common in the early days, it faces the water (Chippewa Creek) rather than Main Street, an indication of the greater importance of travel by water in that time.

Many houses are transitional, having design elements from more than one architectural period. This is particularly true of many of the houses built during the 1830s to 1850s. The simple, rectangular shape of the Greek Revival style and its constant color scheme of pale-painted siding and dark green shutters left little room for individuality. The front doorway served as a focal point and afforded the builder an opportunity for creativity. This Westfield Township house, built in 1835, has the slender, fluted columns and Ionic capitals of the Federal style, yet a heavy entablature and more masculine proportions found in the Greek Revival period.

Peter A. Moore, one of Sharon Township's most important settlers, built this stone Federal in 1839 with additions in 1846 and 1851. Moore was the surveyor for Simon Perkins' vast holdings in Medina County and some of the interior details of this house match those found in the Perkins mansion in Akron. According to the current owners, the smooth-faced ashlar stone for the walls, sills, lintels, and quoins was quarried from a natural arch located on the Moore property.

Barney Prentice's Federal house (the glazed entry doors were a later alteration) was constructed by an early framing method which was already passé in Medina county by 1838 when it was built. Huge hewn timbers support the four corners of the house, similar to today's pole barn construction. The timbers are evident inside by the way the plaster is canted or curved around them. The oldest frame building in the area, David Hudson's 1800 house in Hudson, Summit County, was built in this manner.

The Saltbox House

During the first half of the nineteenth century, Medina County was dotted with small log and Greek Revival houses, with very few other types to alter the view. As late as 1852, 31% of the houses were valued at less than $100, indicating that they were probably log houses or cabins. One variation, however, was the Saltbox house, named for its distinctive roofline which resembled an early wooden salt container. The addition of a lean-to along the rear of a house afforded additional, warm space for a general purpose/bedroom/birthing room. Originating in England and popular in New England, the earliest lean-to addition was an afterthought, but eventually came to be built as part of the original plan. Since this type of house developed on the Eastern seaboard during the seventeenth century, the true Saltbox house is a New England Large or Colonial Farmhouse. The convenient, efficient extension continued to be built into the Greek Revival era, however. Shed-roofed additions were also used on barns and other outbuildings, so that the saltbox or "catslide" profile was a common part of the nineteenth-century landscape. Many Saltbox houses —most dating from the 1830s—can still be found throughout the county.

This Liverpool Township example has a Greek Revival entablature, returns, and belly windows, but the distinctive silhouette of a Saltbox house. The decorative trim and ashlar foundation indicate a well-developed Greek Revival style house despite its modest size.

George Packard's 1846 Saltbox farmhouse in Chatham Township.

Benjamin Agard was born on Long Island, New York, in 1769. He arrived in Wadsworth in 1816, clearing the first fields there in 1818. After the first sawmill in the township was built in 1824, he put up this New England Large house with a saltbox extension which is the oldest frame building in the township.

Clapboarding, paint, and a lean-to addition turned this log house into a Saltbox and changed this homeowner from a pioneer into an established citizen. The angle of the gable roof, lack of foundation, and narrow overhang often indicate the presence of a log cabin under the siding.

Greek Revival

Once the settlers had cleared land for crops and orchards and built barns and outbuildings for animals and food storage, they could turn their energy to building more substantial homes to replace their log cabins or houses. During the era that Medina County was abuilding– about 1830 to the Civil War– the most popular style here and throughout the country was the Greek Revival. First developed in the Eastern states as a rejection of the English styles and a reflection of the democratic ideals of the Greek and Roman city-states, its popularity spread throughout the new nation and endured longer than any other American style. Medina County homeowners who built in the Greek Revival style in the 1830s considered it to be a "modern" style, compared to the Federal or Saltbox or Colonial Farmhouse. Although the Greek Revival style also used Classical elements and a rectangular form, it differed from the Federal in its masculine quality and the use of decorative elements adopted from the Greek temple— a heavy cornice, entablature, and frieze-band, weighty columns, and square, solid proportions. Even a tiny house could resemble a miniature Greek temple with a pediment formed by the gable roof, white or stone-colored paint, returns imitating an entablature and frieze, and columns in the form of flat pilasters flanking the door. The floor plan— boxy rooms laid out around the chimney—continued unchanged without regard for the inhabitants' comfort or needs.

Before the Civil War, construction was post-and-beam using large hewn beams pegged together with "tree nails". Huge logs were stripped of their bark (or it was seared off) to repel insects. The large beams were not only strong, but took less manpower to produce than trimmed ones, as labor was always at a premium on the frontier. Many Medina County homes still have hand-hewn adz marks and bits of bark evident on basement and attic beams.

Wood was, and still is, the most widely used building material in the Western Reserve. It is beautiful, strong, easily worked, and relatively abundant. Greek temples, originally built of wood, were translated into marble at the height of Greek civilization, but the untutored country builder reverted to wood. The charm, attractive proportions, and durability of Greek Revival houses attest to the skill of these early, untrained builders.

The first water-powered sawmill in the county was built by Lathrop Seymour and Timothy Doane in 1817 in Weymouth. Other early sawmills which facilitated building and provided machine-formed materials were constructed in Bagdad in 1818, in Wadsworth in 1824 and in Guilford in 1826.

The exterior color was almost always white with "pleasing-to-the-eye" dark green shutters or blinds. Blinds were in universal use by mid-century to repel insects and protect the glass from storm damage. Moveable louvers were adjusted throughout the day to keep the hot, fading sun off the furnishings. Other exterior colors such as fawn, pale yellow, gray, and cream were known, but the palette was limited to shades which recalled the stone of Greek temples. Contemporary writers, particularly European ones, criticized the monotonous uniformity of these little Greek boxes, but the individuality of the owner or the skill of the builder was exercised in the decoration of the doorway, entablature, or trim. Inside and out, fine details were done by hand. Fluted columns, voluted Ionic capitals, dentil molding, and articulated cornices demonstrate the skill of the frontier carpenter-joiner. Creative, one-of-a-kind designs appear throughout the Western Reserve, but many builders relied upon the designs and patterns illustrated in Minard Lafever's *The Modern Builder's Guide* or Asher Benjamin's *The Architect* or *The Practical House Carpenter.* (The subtitle of which, *Grecian orders of architecture being fashioned according to the styles and practice of the present day*, is telling.) These books were immensely popular during the settlement period of the Reserve, and went into many printings over the next few decades.

Glass, having to be imported, was the single most expensive component of a new building. Small panes—twelve to a sash—are found in some of the earlier and more remote houses but by the end of the Greek Revival era, six-over-six is common. The Western Express shipped goods as far as St. Louis by the 1840s, and local stores were making regular trips to Pittsburgh and other cities for goods, so glass, nails, and hardware were available.

Halsey Hulbert operated one of the county's most active stops on the Underground Railroad in this Greek Revival house in Westfield Township. Fugitive slaves were hidden in a brick enclosure in the cellar which appeared to support the chimney. Access was through a trap door in the first floor. Hulbert came to Westfield in 1830, was a director of the Ohio Farmers' Insurance Company, and served as a township trustee. The Hulbert house was built in 1835.

Charles Franks was born in Wittenburg, Germany and emigrated to Liverpool Township in 1850. In 1857, he built this Greek Revival building which served as house, general store, and stagecoach inn. He dealt in wood, crops, fine breeding stock, and "first class" fertilizer. Two entries separate the residential and commercial functions of the building, now listed on the National Register of Historic Places.

King-Phillips-Deibel House

The King-Phillips-Deible house photographed in its original setting in 1897.

The King-Phillips-Deible house was one of the largest and most handsome Medina County homes. It was built in 1833 by banker, general merchant, and pork dealer David King. He was one of the original investors in the Connecticut Land Company and had extensive holdings in Medina and Montville Townships. He was a man of considerable wealth and wanted a house that reflected it. It is no accident that he selected an imposing site on the southeast corner of the square and built a mansion with a tetra-style porch (a projecting porch supported by four columns) similar to that of the White House. A house of this size and quality, built only fifteen years after the founding of the town, indicates the prosperity of some of Medina's early citizens.

It is believed that the house may have been part of the Underground Railroad. Leicester King of Akron, David's brother, was very active in the abolition movement and ran as vice president under the Liberty Party in 1847.

In 1905, the house was cut into sections and moved from the present site of the Sylvester Library "into the country" about three blocks from the square with all its furnishings intact. According to family history, the move took five days but went so smoothly that there were no plaster cracks and items remained on dresser tops. Teams of horses pulled the house along on railroad ties. After the move, the two-story porches were added and the parlor windows were lengthened to the floor. Fremont Phillips, the owner at the time, bought the electric "light plant" in order to electrify his home, and installed a telephone, but there was no water system and water was still carried from a cistern and a well.

The E.H. Deible family owned the house from 1928 to 1978. It is generally known as the King-Phillips-Deible House in honor of their fifty years of ownership.

George W. Hazen built this Greek Revival farmhouse in Granger Township in 1839. The twelve-over-twelve panes are indicative of the early date for this house. Wooden "shakes" or shingles were generally riven from chestnut in this area. A wonderful picket and hewn stone fence delineates the front of the house and Hazen's monogram adorns the stone buggy step.

Little Greek Revival temples still dot the Western Reserve. When farmer Abel Wood built his temple in Homer Township in 1849, it had a taxable value of $125, the annual wage of a Medina shopkeeper at the time. The nine-over-six pane sash windows are original.

Blake-McDowell House

In 1847, a simple Greek Revival house with a typical trabeated arch and sidelights, wide entablature and returns was built on East Washington Street in Medina. The house changed hands frequently and was altered to suit the needs of its various owners. During the 1850s, an eastern wing was added, giving it a more imposing facade. Harrison G. Blake bought the house in 1855, one year after passage of the Fugitive Slave Act. Under this law, runaway slaves were still considered to be their owner's property even after they had crossed onto free soil. Bounty hunters searched for fugitive slaves and returned them to their Southern owners. Blake was an early opponent of slavery. He supported candidates of the Free Soil party and in the 1850s actively participated in the Underground Railroad movement, a system of safe houses throughout the North in which slaves could find temporary shelter while en route to Canada. Blake may have selected this house for its protective grape arbor leading from the house to the barn. In later years, daughter Elizabeth Blake McDowell spoke of muffled voices and large meals disappearing into the barn. When someone was taking shelter in the home, the Blake children were kept out of school for fear that they might accidentally endanger the fugitives. Mrs. McDowell remembered her father waking her in the middle of the night to meet two fugitive slaves who showed her their scars from repeated beatings.

In 1873, O.C. Shepard, Medina's gristmill owner, bought the house. It is said that he made the money for the house and mill by outfitting prospectors in the California gold fields. The family has letters and a little gold dust to verify the story. The Shepards raised seven children here, adding rooms for their growing family in 1876. Granddaughter Pauline Griesinger McClelland lived here until the 1980s. For over one hundred years, this house was home to members of the Shepard and Griesinger families. Mrs. McClelland recalled huge trees that arched over East Washington Street and open ditch storm sewers. The barn that harbored fugitives made a great play area until her brother Charles fell from the loft and went into a deep coma. The doctor ordered all church bells to be silenced and diverted buggy traffic so that Charles could wake up naturally. He did, and lived into his nineties.

The Blake/McDowell house has seen many changes and additions but is a prime example of a basic Greek Revival house adapted to the needs of subsequent owners. It remains as one of Medina's most historically significant homes, and has been placed on the National Register of Historic Places.

A detail drawing from Asher Benjamin's pattern book, *The Practical House Carpenter*.

The builder of the Simmons house in Westfield Township must have been familiar with architect Asher Benjamin's work. Copies of *The Practical House Carpenter* are known to have existed in the county.

Usual woods for fine hand carving were close-grained cherry, walnut, and maple, which held a clean, sharp edge. The Greek key or fret design is a common Classical motif. A glazed transom and sidelights let light into the windowless entryway. The house has been in the Simmons family since it was built in 1847.

The *anthemion*, or honeysuckle, was a Greek Revival motif found in Asher Benjamin's work and other early nineteenth-century pattern books. The *guttae*, the small, drop-like ornaments, are individually carved. This house, built in 1859, is well off the beaten path in Spencer Township, yet the owner obviously took great pride in his home and the detailing is lovely. This exact anthemion is found in four other houses in the area, giving some credence to the theory that they all may have been built by Lorain County carpenter O.T. Baker.

This Harrisville Township house, which at first glance is a rather common Greek Revival farmhouse, merits closer inspection. The builder was evidently a carpenter of some skill. The entire front face of the house, under the full-facade porch, is paneled. This type of paneling, or wainscoting, was developed for its strength (a wain is a wagon, built to hold heavy loads). It is made of individual parts which can shrink or expand with the changes in atmosphere without cracking or separating. Although rare in the Western Reserve, a porch like this does exist in nearby Homer Township. The Doric columns have a slight convex swelling, or *entasis*, which was developed by the ancient Greeks. This swelling of the shaft makes it appear that the column is bearing the weight of the porch, and prevents it from looking weak and spindly. A carpenter working in the Ohio countryside in the mid nineteenth century must have had access to architectural pattern books to be aware of illusionary building techniques developed by ancient civilizations.

A five-bay facade and emphasized, central door closely align this brick house to the Federal style. The heavy entablature, side and transom lights, American bonding, and late date (1845) place it in the Greek Revival period. The door has a marquetry tree-of-life design. Lemuel Smith, a prosperous Westfield Township farmer, was the first owner.

Dr. A.L. Simmons built this brick house in Wadsworth Township in 1853-55. It is one of the many Wadsworth Township farmhouses located at the end of long lanes, far removed from the road. The Greek Revival house has a fanlight carried over from the Federal period. In addition to his farm and orchard, Simmons had a forty-acre seam of "top quality" bituminous coal on his farm, and was mining two hundred tons a day in 1874. Simmons and his wife raised nine children in this house.

This impressive Greek Revival house on Sharon Circle is one of the most well-known houses in the county. It was built by postmaster Luther Fitch about 1850 for a taxable value of $320. The two-story porch and balusters were added at the turn of the twentieth century when the country was going through another revival of Greek architecture.

John Kennedy and his family settled in Medina Township in 1838 and lived in a log cabin while clearing their land and establishing their crops. It took eighteen years to move into this fine brick example of the Greek Revival style. According to family history, itinerant carpenter Joe Henry lived with the family in the cabin for one year while he built this house for the Kennedys. He was paid one hundred silver dollars, room, board, and his tobacco supply.

The Sargent house, a brick, hip-roofed example of the Greek Revival style, was built in Medina Village about 1854. The doorway, made of pilasters supporting an architrave and segmented transom window, is particularly handsome. The frieze-band windows have decorative iron grills, allowing light into the top half-story but protecting the owner's privacy. Drip molding was known in early architecture, but the delicate proportions of this example indicate that it was a Victorian addition. The two-over-two windows would be found after about 1870.

Stone houses are rare in the Western Reserve, particularly in Medina County. John Gargett, an English immigrant, bought 120 acres in Hinckley Township for four dollars per acre and built this Saltbox house for himself in the 1840s. He was a stone mason who purportedly helped to build the Simon Perkins mansion in Akron, as well as the Peter Moore house in Sharon Township. Thousands of chisel marks are evident on the hand-hewn stones. Gargett died in 1884 in the Hinckley Township house he "built with his own hands, lo these many years ago", and in which he and his wife raised nine children.

This Liverpool Center (now Valley City) house may have been used as a coaching station. Its builder creatively cut the dentils out of long boards, rather than piecing each one individually. The cornice and pediment trim of the columned porch are heavily articulated. Unfortunately, this fine example of the vernacular Greek Revival style was razed in 1977.

York Township "Greeks"

York Township was established late in the settlement history of the county. The area was advertised to Easterners as being rich and fertile with a high turnpike road opened through it. In fact, the land was swampy and there was no road at all. It was not until 1830 that the township was opened to settlement and the first cabin built. While nearby Medina Village and area townships were putting up their permanent Federal and Greek Revival houses, settlers in York Township were just beginning to build their rude, temporary log cabins. The proximity to store-bought goods allowed them to progress quickly, however. A sawmill went up in Mallet Creek in 1835 and soon after in Lester which allowed permanent building to begin.

The five wonderful Greek Revival houses flanking Norwalk and Fenn Roads were all built about the same time (1846) and all were valued for taxes at about $250. Each one is situated on a little knoll with its long facade to the street, and their handsome appearance and large scale present a striking view. Each has carefully executed architectural details and is as attractive on the side views as the front. The addition of such beautiful houses to the area increased nearby land values and caused prices to escalate.

Unfortunately, two other fine examples were razed in 1994.

Standing on a hill overlooking Norwalk Road, this house built for Thompson Pierce is one of the finest examples of Greek Revival architecture in the county.

According to local history, these two Norwalk Road houses were built by an itinerant carpenter. He first built a log cabin on the property and lived there while he was putting up the houses and completing the hand-finished woodwork and the staircases inside.

Valley City "Greeks"

Several houses in the vicinity of Valley City are notable because of their brick construction. According to one of the early owners, they were not built by the same carpenter, but rather were the happy result of a brick company in town. They were all built during the late 1850s and 1860s, a time when the Civil War interrupted most construction in the county. The houses are all of the Greek Revival or Western Reserve style, with bricks laid in common or American bond (that is, with the long or stretcher ends exposed), and stone sills and lintels. Most of the houses have little adornment except for some decorative interest at the doorway. White or pale-painted wooden doors and trim add interest to the dark, brick walls.

The Carl Betz house on State Route 303 photographed in the 1960s.

The Carl Betz home as it looks today.

These three brick houses on Route 303 in Valley City and Liverpool Township were all built around 1860. Like others of their type in the area, they are all Greek Revival or Western Reserve in style.

Western Reserve

As the Western Reserve grew, it developed its own distinct version of the Greek Revival style. It is a one-and-a-half story house with the temple facade or gable end to the street and a small ell to one or both sides. This style is familiarly known as the "upright and wing". Often there was a small porch *in antis* or inset into the ell behind columns. The result is a less formal and elegant building, but one which was well suited to the needs of the settlers. Western Reserve houses can be found in Ohio, Michigan, Illinois, Indiana, and Kentucky where New Englanders settled at the beginning of the nineteenth century. These houses are still very common throughout Medina County, where a large percentage of the citizens had emigrated from New England. The Western Reserve house, like the Greek Revival, was typically painted white, putty, sand, or some other pale color imitating stone, with blinds (shutters with moveable louvers) in dark green. In the small half-story attic, the roof was too shallow for a full-sized window. At any rate, only the gable walls were tall enough to accommodate beds. As a result, tiny windows were placed in the small space between the floor and the roof. These little windows are known as "belly" or "lie-on-your-belly" windows. They were often the only source of light into the upper story, and ventilated a space that would have been stifling in the summer months.

A Hinckley Township farmhouse at the end of the nineteenth century.

The front door of this Granger Township Western Reserve house is offset to allow more space for the parlor. Although used only on Sundays and special occasions, the parlor or "front room" was the most important room in the house as it indicated the refinement and culture of the owners.

Local carpenters often made use of the Doric order of Greek architecture. The flat pieces forming the pilasters, capital, and entablature of this Weymouth house could be sawn from wood stock and then hand-planed. More decorative elements such as Ionic or Corinthian capitals necessitated hand carving. The Doric order is also simpler in that the column does not rest on a base.

Small windows in the frieze band are known as "belly" or "lie-on-your-belly windows". They let light and air into the small upper half-story and were common in Western Reserve houses. Tiny shutters like these are unusual but charming. Thomas and Rebeckah Palmer built this little house in 1832. Orrin and Lydia Gridley of Medina bought the property in 1849 and farmed it until Orrin's death in 1882.

Burritt Blakeslee came to Weymouth from Waterbury, Connecticut in 1816. He was a skilled carpenter who built many houses in the area and this one for himself. It was built in 1855 after a fire destroyed his first home. Although it is unclear how he learned his craft, it is known that he had a copy of Asher Benjamin's *Practical House Carpenter*. Writing of Blakeslee in *Early Homes of Ohio*, I.T. Frary says, "With limited means and the simplest of tools and equipment they lavished the finest of workmanship on their houses, producing mouldings, paneling and other details that put to shame most of the work that is done today. The builder took a pride in his work that permitted him to do nothing but the best his tools and ability made possible."

Monitors

The "monitor" on these houses may have been merely a design element, or may have developed from the old defensive blockhouses which had overhanging second stories. It was clearly not named after the famous Confederate iron-clad warship, since houses of this type existed prior to 1860. Perhaps both house and ship were named for the fact that the extended upper story provides a lookout from which to "monitor" events.

The monitor house is considered by some to be a corruption of the "upright and wing" Western Reserve house. The temple facade has become a large dormer and the ells have joined to become the first floor of the house. This Westfield Township house has an *in antis* porch and little decoration except for its heavy Greek entablature and doorway. It was built in 1853 by Abraham Walcott, the local miller.

This house was built in 1838 for William Sausaman, a director of the Ohio Farmers' Insurance Company. It was the first brick house in Westfield Township, the bricks having been fired on the site. The enclosed pedimented porch was added in the twentieth century.

Schools

The pioneer families who migrated to Medina County understood the value of education for their children. One of their first communal tasks was to build a log school house, which often served as church and community center as well. These primitive schools were only about sixteen by eighteen feet in area. The floors were puncheon and the few tiny windows were greased paper. Pegs driven into the logs under the windows, with another puncheon resting across them, served as a desk for writing lessons near the only source of light. Students sat on split logs with pegged legs.

There were no text books, and the Bible served as a reader. A young local woman might teach with an English reader or math book that she brought from the East. The instructors were the sons and daughters of early pioneers who stayed with their own families or "boarded around" with the families of pupils. The pay was about one dollar per week, assessed from the families with school-age children.

Many were opposed to the idea of using public funds to train teachers or to support schools. As a result, much early education took place in private institutions. There were four systems: academies, normal, select, and public schools. Academies offered general education. Normal schools for teacher education and commercial training were private, expensive, and controlled by a board of trustees. There were academies in Lodi, Wadsworth and Seville and a normal school in Medina. Select schools were also private but were managed as well as taught by the instructor. William P. Clark had a select school in Medina in 1847 and a Miss Lee taught young ladies in a private school on East Liberty Street. Children who could not afford private schools attended small, public township schools financed by assessment. Their education was limited and, until the end of the century, rarely went beyond the eighth grade level.

Medina was the first village to press for better public education. In 1872, school board members began construction of Medina High School at South Broadway and Smith Roads. By 1881 there were high schools in Lodi, Hinckley, Granger, Sharon, Chatham, Wadsworth, Seville, Weymouth, and LeRoy. The one-room schoolhouse still served the townships with students attending winter and summer sessions from grades one through eight. Spring and fall were reserved for planting and harvesting. By the end of the century, property taxes funded schools for all, but until then it was not uncommon for parents to pay their children's tuition in firewood or labor.

The early teachers were neither trained nor certified. Few were much more educated or even much older than their pupils. Their single qualification was that they could read and cipher. In 1834 the County finally appointed a Board of Examiners to impose educational standards. In 1847, the Medina County Teacher's Institute opened in the courthouse.

The schools, like the churches, were gathering spots for the small communities. Recitations, plays, concerts, bees, and holiday celebrations were held in the schools, which served as social centers until the 1920s. Communities indicated their pride in these schools by papering, "graining" and painting them inside and out, and hanging prints of famous paintings. With the advent of the automobile and school bus, students were transported to centrally located schools and the one-room schoolhouse disappeared. Many were abandoned, while others were relocated to became outbuildings or were converted into homes that are still occupied.

Medina County's only octagon public building was a frame school in the Greek Revival style built in 1839 on the present site of Wadsworth's Reformed Church. It had a domed octagonal cupola with a pinnacle and a roofed entrance with a pedimented gable and free-standing columns. Doric pilasters delineate the eight corners of the building.

John McGregor, an educator from Scotland, took control of the school upon its completion in 1839 and operated it as an academy for higher education until 1846. It remained vacant until 1861 when the Reformed Church bought it for $150 and referred to it as the "round church". When the congregation put up a new building in 1873, the octagon was moved to Lyman and Prospect Streets where it served as the Evangelical church, and was later razed.

This small school is evidently an early one, although its date is unclear. Originally, it was located at the corner of Marks and Sleepy Hollow Roads on the John Frank farm. Although it appears in the 1874 county atlas, there is no record of the land having been deeded to the Liverpool Board of Education. Perhaps it was one of the schools closed during the 1898 diphtheria epidemic. The six-over-six paned windows are an indication that the school was built prior to the 1860s. The standing-seam tin roof is a replacement, but the cloak room and slate chalkboard remain inside.

Joseph Northrop was one of the first settlers in Medina Township, arriving in 1816. He cleared a farm in the area known as Northrop-ville at the crossing of Nettleton and Granger(burgh) roads. This school was built on his property. It was the only public building in an area of pioneer farms and was the center of the community. It was built by N.B. Northrop from July to December, 1848. He was paid $150 for the school and the stove, and the total cost for the building, furnishings, and paint was $205.33. The school opened with the summer session (May to September) with four girls and nine boys aged five to fifteen. The teacher, Frances E. Cook, was paid fifteen dollars for fifteen weeks' work. Winter sessions met for three months and the teacher's pay was forty dollars. She taught the students orthography (spelling), reading, writing, arithmetic, grammar, geography, philosophy, astronomy, algebra, and botany. In 1854, there were forty-nine pupils in this tiny one-room schoolhouse.

Built in 1865, this little frame schoolhouse represents the standard size and design for the county. The distinctive feature is the decorative slate roof and bell cupola with "no. 6" visible in the slate. Even though the school was located on the Newcomer farm in Wadsworth Township, it was known as the Wright School after Ephriam Wright's farm across Wall Street. This school still stands on its original site and is now used as an outbuilding.

School #10 in Lafayette was built in the Stick Style in 1885 for $1025. The bell tower was especially handsome and indicates the pride that local citizens took in their schools.

LeRoy Village created its own school district in 1872 and built this fine frame building in 1873. It had a classroom and teacher for each grade level–primary, intermediate, and high–plus a large hall for public exercises. It cost $8000, a sum raised in part through the efforts of A.G. Hawley, the secretary of Ohio Farmers' Insurance.

The ornate acanthus-leaf ancones or corbels flanking the door are heavier than necessary to support the bracketed pediment, but with the four-story bell tower and pedimented windows, are a decorative embellishment that would have been a source of pride for the community.

One of Medina County's most impressive academic buildings was first conceived in a Lodi town meeting in 1867. An advanced school was needed for the growing student population. O.S. Kinney was hired to design a brick and stone Second Empire style building with three stories, concave mansard roofs, and a four-story bell tower. A stone foundation, decorative chimneys, paired windows, and stone lintels and keystones add interest. In 1871, the $26,000 school opened. A frame dormitory which still stands served 120 out-of-town students. As public schools improved, enrollment declined and in 1879 the Lodi school board bought the academy building for $5000 for use as a public school. Elementary classes were free, but tuition was charged for the upper grades. In 1925, the grand brick building was razed.

This two-story schoolhouse in Weymouth was built about 1860. A smaller Greek Revival building at the opposite end of town on Remsen Road served the primary grades, and advanced students were taught here. The second floor, reached by the rear staircase, housed Weymouth's Sons of Temperance hall. The school is used today as a residence and except for the loss of its belfry, is little altered.

Throughout the nineteenth century, communities agitated for better and more thorough education for their children. The high school movement in Medina County began in 1871 in Medina Village. By the end of the century, there were twelve high schools in the county, including this one at Chippewa Lake, photographed about 1910.

Not long after its initial settlement, Wadsworth became the home of a large Mennonite population, primarily from Pennsylvania. This German-American group was so strong that in 1863 Wadsworth was chosen as the site of a "Christian Education Institute of the Mennonite Denomination", the only one of its kind in the United States. Completed in 1865 for the considerable fee of $17,000, the Mennonite College building was designed by Aaron Kent of Pennsylvania. Wadsworth businessman Ephriam Hunsberger donated the land at the geographical center of the township. The impressive three-story brick building, 60 by 38 feet in area, was a simple rectangle adorned with a three-story cupola and octagonal bell tower. Even though it was a Mennonite school, it was open to all. Tuition was $100 per year for instruction, board, "fuel, washing, and light". Christian Showalter of Iowa was the first principal, and three teachers led classes. After only ten years of operation, the college closed when a split divided the Mennonite community. For some years a normal school occupied the building and trained teachers for area schools. After 1892, the Wadsworth board of education purchased this building for a high school and it became the first Centralized School of Wadsworth when the one-room township schools ceased to operate in 1915. In 1923, the old Mennonite College building was razed to make room for a new twelve-room school.

Gothic Revival

After decades of somber Greek Revival architecture, more decorative styles began to pave the way toward the eccentric variety found during the Victorian Era.

The Gothic Revival style was first adopted as an ecclesiastical one, when church architects and leaders began to realize that the pagan Greco-Roman ideals were not appropriate for Christian worship. Many of the elements of Medieval European cathedrals—vertical emphasis, lancet windows, buttresses, and masonry construction—were translated into nineteenth-century Gothic Revival village churches. By mid-century, architect and landscape gardener Andrew Jackson Downing was designing Gothic "cottage residences" for rural settings.

William Harrison Seymour built his house (next page) in 1851. It has Gothic detailing—lancet windows, tri-partite porch columns, drip molding over windows and doors, tall, peaked multiple gables, "gingerbread" carved vergeboards, and Tudor arches. Each porch column has three lobes, representing the Trinity. Stripped of its Gothic decoration, however, it is a traditional square farmhouse. Except for the steep and multiple Gothic gables, all of the trim is superficial. Even the lancet windows are non-functional, decorative trim for the traditional six-over-six sashes. Originally, two front doors entered into the family and Sunday parlors, extending the symmetry of the house. The chimney passes through the attic at an angle so that it can be symmetrically placed in the center of the roof. The large "picture" window was added to update the house after it was struck by a tornado in 1932.

Typically, the Gothic Revival style building employs board-and-batten siding to emphasize verticality, but this version translates wood into "stone" by using seamless boards laid flush under the porch and off-white body paint.

Given that the Medina landscape in 1851 was dotted with log houses and Western Reserve examples of the Greek Revival style, this house must have seemed very fanciful and contemporary when it was built. Seymour was educated in the East and no doubt became familiar with new styles of architecture while at school. His house is the earliest example of the Gothic Revival style in the area, foreshadowing the picturesque, decorative styles soon to be popular throughout the country.

Seymour House was built by timber frame or post-and-beam construction, hand-planed lumber, and hand-wrought nails and hardware in 1851, when urban areas were making use of new tools and materials. Industrialization did not effectively alter Medina County building until after the Civil War.

In 1874, Weymouth native Norton W. Welton bought this house and retired to it from Denver, Colorado, a city which he helped to settle. He had gone West as a young man to find his fortune and in eleven years had a 4420 acre estate valued at $40,000. He must have been homesick, however, because he returned to Weymouth, married his stepsister, and bought the Seymour House which he had known as a boy. Although Welton modernized the house by adding a bay window and a kitchen and painting it bright "crushed carrots" orange, the house is little altered from his day and is listed on the National Register.

Charles (front) and Susie (second from left) Edwards in front of Seymour house about 1916. They were the owners from 1907 until 1948. The pine tree, planted to commemorate the completion of the house in 1851, still stands. The iron fence is signed *Dann* and has a stone foundation three feet deep. Separate front doors opened into the family and company parlors.

A detail of one of the houses' seven gables shows the blind lancet window and the hand-carved vergeboards. The deep overhang not only protects the windows from the weather, but allows the gingerbread to cast a decorative shadow.

Churches

Medina County's settlers came from the East—Connecticut, New York, Massachusetts—to start a new life. They were Christians who sought means to worship and understood the value of education for their children. At first, they gathered in log homes, read scripture and prayed for the arrival of the first minister. In some cases they built a separate log cabin solely for the purpose of worship and education.

Not only the religious appreciated the need for the stabilizing influence of organized worship in the community. It is interesting to note that of the nine charter members who founded St. Paul's parish, only two were communicants.

As forests disappeared and the population expanded, congregations sought to build more substantial houses of worship. In Medina County, where congregations grew slowly, the classic white clapboard church did not appear until the 1830s. By this time, sawmills dotted the area, making milled lumber available for building on a larger scale. For the Yankees transplanted in Medina County, the natural style for these early churches was the Federal or Greek Revival and the natural material was wood. These classic designs harkened back to the temples of Greece and served well as a temple of worship in the new land. With its symmetry and rectangular basilica plan, the Greek Revival church was starkly formal, but local congregations embellished their churches with porticoes, belfries, cornice and entrance details, according to their financial means. After the Civil War, the country grew into a new industrial era, and the old passion for the ideals of Greco-Roman society waned. A new ecclesiastical architecture, more appropriate to Christian worship, became popular. Architects and church leaders looked to the highly religious Middle Ages for new design inspiration. The simple, white-painted Greek Revival churches, solidly anchored to the ground, gave way to the masonry construction and vertical emphasis of the Gothic Revival style. Some of the early churches were razed or relocated to serve as barns or shops and the new Gothic Revival church took its place.

In Medina County, all Greek Revival churches were wood frame, but the Victorian churches used wood, brick and stone. This was particularly true in the northwest part of the county where a community of German immigrants built a number of fine brick churches which are indicative of their building skills and their faith.

With a vestibule or narthex at one end of the sanctuary and a chancel or altar at the other, the standard rectangular plan became more complex. A spire or steeple with a belfry served as a religious symbol and as a new design element. Steep gables and pointed arches added to the vertical, uplifting effect. Spires rose from the ground, not the roof, to add vertical emphasis. These tall churches towered over the fields and villages and served as a focal point and source of pride of the community. Of particular charm is the vernacular country church. Often the small, rural congregations could not afford the elaborate designs of the Victorian Gothic when the Greek Revival style was no longer in vogue. They adapted features from the new style, adding a spire or lancet windows and bringing their simple frame churches into the Victorian era.

Churches from the simple log to the fine stone Gothic served equally well as the community center for the neighborhood. Weddings and funerals were generally held at home, but weekly services, Sunday School, revivals, and holiday pageants attracted people in a time when travel was often difficult and social contact was limited.

According to an account in the 1881 *History of Medina County*, the development of the area churches was not without difficulty. When the first pioneer families came west, they carried the heavy burden of a strict, Puritan faith of New England. But in the woods, on their own, they became "free thinkers" and gave up strict sectarianism for a philosophy based on common sense. If a person had character and honesty, his or her religious beliefs were of little consequence. In the early years of the county faiths worshipped together, but as the area prospered and permanent churches were built, the old schisms between the denominations returned. There were also divisions within the congregations. The Lutheran church in Valley City separated when a group felt some in the church were not practicing "true Lutheranism". Prior to the Civil War, other congregations divided over the slavery issue. The "free thinkers" or abolitionists won out and those churches that had split over the issue reunited.

Today many of the county's historic church buildings survive. Some house the original denomination, while others host new groups. Others have undergone additions and alterations which demonstrate a change in design attitudes and congregational needs. Medina County's nineteenth-century churches remain an important part of our architectural heritage.

The Universalist sect sought to nurture the mind as well as the spirit. They championed many causes: abolition, prohibition, and universal peace. They first gathered in Sharon Center in 1830, but did not build a church until 1851. The congregation flourished for many years but in 1937 their redundant church was desanctified and dedicated to Sharon Township for use as a township hall. The wheat sheaf fanlight, a hold-over from the Federal period, and Doric-columned tower are especially fine.

Built in 1842, this Federal church now known as St. Marks' Episcopal has seen a number of occupants. Congregationalists, with their strong New England roots, built it from a design by George Hinsdale, a local joiner-carpenter. There have been few changes through the years, apart from the addition of a belfry, and St. Mark's is listed on the National Register of Historic Places.

As Wadsworth grew, it underwent a shift in population. Pennsylvania Dutch settlers moved into the area and eventually outnumbered the early New England settlers. In 1885, the Congregationalists disbanded and in 1892 the Mennonites moved in. At this time, the Mennonites were a leading group and had three churches in Wadsworth Township and a seminary which welcomed students of all faiths. They worshipped here into the twentieth century.

Doric responds on the face of the building reflect four Doric columns supporting a tetra-style full facade porch. The hand-carved wheat sheaf lunette or fanlight window in the pedimented gable is characteristic of the Federal style. The belfry's columns complement those of the portico.

When the Chatham Congregational Church was organized in 1834, it was incorporated under the Presbyterian covenant. Like other Congregationalists in the county, they later separated from Presbyterian control and formed a separate entity. As a result, competition between the two denominations was strong and they never built churches in the same community. In 1844 the Chatham congregation subscribed $700 in pew subscriptions to build their first church. The transitional Federal/Greek Revival building was completed in 1846. Six years later the members bought a bell for four hundred dollars and added a belfry and entrance to the gable end of the building. In 1874, Walter Fleming improved the interior with blue "tint" paper and a cornice, and leaded glass windows brought the church into the Victorian age.

The Chatham Congregationalists consistently championed the cause of freedom. There was a strong anti-slavery movement within the church and at least two members operated Underground Railroad stations from their homes.

Churches in New England were closely based upon the work of English architects Christopher Wren and James Gibbs. In turn, churches on the Western Reserve followed the example and were built with a rectangular basilica shape, white clapboard siding, a spire rising but slightly set back from the roofline, a symmetrical facade, and Classical details and proportions.

The Seville Presbyterians organized in 1811 and had an earlier church prior to this Greek Revival one built in 1856. James Whiteside and George Cook of Seville were the contractors. When it was dedicated in 1857, it was the largest church in town, accommodating three hundred worshippers.

Weymouth Church in 1937.

In January of 1835, a small band of Congregationalists met at the Weymouth home of member Lathrop Seymour to plan the incorporation and construction of their church. They purchased a lot for forty-five dollars from Timothy Doane and the men of the church began to build their Greek Revival edifice. By summer they held services in the "enclosure" that was partially complete. In 1853, pews were taxed to raise funds for Elijah Tiffany to add a belfry and pro-style porch to the facade. The Doric columns are repeated on the belfry and its cornice, frieze and architrave form a classical entablature. In 1875 the youth of the church raised funds for a new bell by performing plays at the Weymouth School. Such activities were not permitted in the meeting house.

Prior to the Civil War when other congregations split over the slavery issue, the Weymouth Congregationalists passed a resolution urging the Medina County Presbytery to denounce slavery. When the Presbytery refused in 1846, the Weymouth Church voted to remove itself from the ruling body.

After World War I, the congregation dwindled, and the building has housed the Weymouth Community Church Society since 1920.

Founded in 1838, the Granger Disciples did not have a church building until 1862 when Benjamin Low leased them the land for public worship. They built this very simple Greek Revival church known as the East Granger Disciples Church. The two entrance doors separating the sexes are original and lead into a cloak room. Shingles cover the original narrow clapboards and tall windows. Sometime before 1890, the congregation disbanded and those remaining joined the Disciples Church at Remsen Corners. The building is now a private residence.

Organized in 1882, the congregation of the Remsen Church met in the GAR Hall just south of Remsen Corners and began to build this country frame church. Completed in 1893, it cost $1575 for both the lot and the building. The simple basilica or rectangular plan has an attached bell tower entrance. The roundel represents the stained glass rose window of a Gothic cathedral. Turned posts and gingerbread trim in the upper belfry are popular Victorian elements. In 1923, the GAR hall was moved and attached to the rear of the church for use as offices and Sunday School rooms.

The Congregational Church, organized in 1819, is one of the oldest in the county. Early services were held in log cabins in Bagdad and Medina Village alternately. In 1832, a brick church was built in Medina, replaced by this Gothic Revival church in 1882. In 1931, the dark Victorian woodwork, walls, and pews were updated with white paint.

Emmanuel Church is part of the German legacy in Liverpool Township. The first home of the congregation was a log church situated south of the Center, but differences in doctrine forced a small splinter group to leave and form the Emmanuel Church. This 1869 building replaces a smaller, earlier structure. Other groups later merged with the congregation, which became known as the Emmanuel United Church of Christ. The plain gable-front brick church has its original double paneled doors with a stained glass lunette. A rose window is tucked under the eaves. The octagonal steeple with its arched belfry is unique in Medina County.

Moses Parsons came into Medina County as a staunch Methodist. By 1832, he had gathered enough Methodists in the area to ride with the Wellington circuit ministers. In 1850 this small band joined with a group from the northern part of the township and built a frame church. When it burned in 1853, it was replaced by the present structure just north of town center. At this time, the choir sat in the balcony at the rear of the church and each time they sang a hymn, the congregation rose and turned to face them. The Chatham Methodist Church is a Greek Revival building with a unique, asymmetrically-placed belfry added in 1852. The pagoda tower, a later alteration, is crowned with a steeple with flared eaves, now roofed with standing-seamed tin. Another alteration was the addition of a school building relocated from district #4 to the rear of the church. The building underwent restorations in 1869 and 1944. Blind windows in the belfry were covered over in the 1990s. The windows are slightly pointed, and bracketed hood moldings throw rain away from the simple rectangular windows.

This Homer Township church began as the Evangelical Reformed Church in 1836. Services were conducted in German and held first in a log cabin and then in a frame building on Pawnee Road. In 1859, a split occurred in the congregation and one group formed the Zion Lutheran Church. The original body remained in their early church but in the 1890s began to conduct services in English as well as German. In 1895, the Reformed congregation erected this new church. Built with local labor, this frame church has a steep gable roof accented with fishscale shingles and a small triangular stained glass window. The side tower has an open belfry with a balustrade and Victorian trim work. The four paneled doors with stained glass "Welcome" windows are original. The building is now the home of the East Homer United Church of Christ.

Mallet Creek's lovely Victorian village church was designed and built by Thomas Rogers, an illiterate but able builder. The steep gable roof and central spire are accentuated with decorative brickwork which frames the architectural details. The rounded door and window arches and double louvered belfry are capped with brick. Stepped buttresses with stone tops and arcaded hood molding over the windows add interest to the irregular outline. Modern stained glass replaces the original "stained obscured ornamental glass".

The land was donated by Richard Lampson under the provision that it would revert to his heirs if no longer used as a church. Another major benefactor was "Aunt Mary" Ford, who gave $3000 of the $7000 needed for the building and appointments. For this generous gift and her many good works, York United Methodist Church was known as "Mary's Chapel".

Founded in 1817, Medina's St. Paul's parish began in a primitive log cabin, built in a day. In the 1850s, the congregation built a Greek Revival frame church in Medina Village. In 1882, plans were drawn up for a new structure. Member Hiram Bronson, a prominent Medina businessman, agreed to increase his pledge if the church were built of stone. Gordon W. Lloyd, a noted church architect from Detroit, was hired to design the Gothic Revival building. The church vestry accepted David Robertson's bid of $11,000 to build the church. Robertson had proven himself with his work on the Ohio Farmers' Insurance Building at LeRoy. On April 14, 1884, two hundred members and well-wishers gathered for the laying of the cornerstone and construction began. By October 1885, the Grafton stone church was almost complete. Another memorial subscription raised $2300 for stained glass windows imported from Germany. Hiram Bronson donated $700 for the stunning window depicting St. Paul preaching on Mars Hill. Finally, on December 19, the first service was held in Medina County's only stone church. The old building was moved to the corner of Court and Friendship Streets for A.B. Bishop's carriage factory. A turn-of-the-century parish hall and a sensitive 1960s addition are the only changes to the fine church, listed on the National Register of Historic Places.

In 1840, a group of German Catholic families from Abbeyville visited Bishop Purcell of Cincinnati and convinced him of their need for a parish church in Liverpool Township. They founded St. Martin of Tours six years before the Diocese of Cleveland was established. Originally, the small group built two log churches on each side of the Rocky River so that high water would not interrupt services. A rivalry developed between the two groups, but when the two little buildings were outgrown, they banded together to build a brick church on the west side of the river. By 1860, they outgrew this building as well and hired architect Patrick C. Kelly to design this fine brick church. Each man in the congregation gave one year to its construction of bricks fired from local clay. The shell was completed by 1861, but it took twenty years to finish the elaborate interior. In 1872, statues and a hand-carved altar arrived from Germany and the interior was painted in a palette of six colors. In 1881, the large pipe organ was installed and in 1897, stained glass replaced the original plain green glass windows. St. Martin's incorporates European design and craftsmanship. Arched doors and windows, buttresses, and a steep roof are typical Gothic Revival characteristics. The beautiful 164-foot tower rises impressively in the center of the Liverpool countryside.

When the German Lutherans first organized in Liverpool Township in 1834, they dreamed of building a church. This became possible in 1838 when Nathan Carr donated an acre of land. The first church was a two-story frame one with a bell tower and simple Greek Revival details. In 1894-1897 that building was replaced by the present Gothic Revival church, known as *Evangehlischl Lutherniche Zions Kirchen Gemende*, situated on an imposing hill on Abbeyville Road. The design of this church is very similar to nearby St. Martin's. The 107-foot tower rises up from the ground and has pinnacles at each corner, adding to the vertical emphasis. Buttresses and lancet windows add to the uplifting effect. There are three bells in the tower to call the faithful to worship.

Cemeteries

When the first settlers came into Medina County, of course, there were no dedicated burial grounds. In Weymouth, Lathrop Seymour buried his wife in an existing burial plot used by Native Americans. Most families laid their loved ones to rest on the homestead property. Some of these small family burial plots have been sadly obliterated by time and development, but others remain today marked with leaning stones and spreading myrtle.

Once there was a small community of settlers and the little churches were raised, churchyard cemeteries were dedicated by congregations. This is particularly true of German communities in Liverpool, Wadsworth, and Homer townships where the German tradition of churchyard burials continued.

In other small villages and hamlets, benefactors gave land expressly for the use of a public cemetery. In 1818, Elijah Boardman set aside some land at the edge of Medina Village for the Old Town Cemetery. Wedged between the Congregational and Episcopal churches, this plot was used in Medina Village until Spring Grove Cemetery opened in 1884. During this time, Liberty Street was called Graveyard Road and the deceased were carried to their graves by horse-drawn bier while the church bells tolled out their ages.

Toward the end of the nineteenth century, new, progressive cemetery designs came into the county. This rural cemetery movement gained favor during the Civil War when President Lincoln dedicated Gettysburg Cemetery as a monument to those who died nearby. It was planned to escape the gloom of the churchyard and create a garden for the living as well as the dead. As they watched the passing of the seasons, mourners found comfort in the healing process and the rebirth of nature's own cycle. Thus, cemeteries became parks– a shrine to the dead and a comfort to the living. Spring Grove in Medina, Woodlawn in Lodi and Wadsworth, and Mound Hill Cemetery in Seville were developed under the influence of the cemetery movement. Small ponds, wandering paths, fountains, decorative iron fences and stately trees provided a park-like setting and attracted picnickers and strollers. The gravestones themselves became works of art—sculptures in a garden. Cemeteries became a source of community pride. Landscape architects and cemetery designers were hired to aid the community in the design of these showplaces.

When Spring Grove Cemetery was dedicated in 1884, there were orations and performances of choral music in celebration. Some people moved their family member's remains from the Old Town cemetery to the new one. The *Gazette* told of a Mr. Johnson who was exhumed after ten year's burial and transported to his new resting place. Mr. Johnson had been interred in a Victorian casket which had a window over the face area to insure that the occupant was truly dead. When Johnson was moved, it attracted a crowd and many comments as to his fine appearance after ten years under ground.

Early burial grounds in Medina County were plagued by illegal "resurrectionsists". It was difficult for doctors to acquire suitable subjects for medical research. Experiments were done on the unclaimed poor or graves robbed during the night. In Wadsworth in the 1840s, Dr. George Pardee operated a medical college at Broad and Lyman Streets. Many suspected that his cadavers came from Woodlawn Cemetery. Prior to 1850, the cemetery was poorly cared for and high grass and sumac trees obscured the gravestones, providing cover for grave robbers.

In 1875 in Montville Township, Tom King died and was buried in the potter's field at the County Infirmary. Dr. Hudson of Medina thought that King was an excellent candidate for research because of his "emaciated condition" and proceeded to disinter his remains, with the help of two assistants. Just as they began, someone shot at the group and Dr. Hudson was hit. The others quickly scattered. For an hour, Hudson wandered around blind until he stumbled into a neighboring house. He lost an eye and everyone in town knew of his crime. Many feared that the same fate might befall their loved ones. Friends and family members stood guard over new graves and stone mausoleums were built to protect the dead.

Hinckley's Maple Hill Cemetery vault was built in 1885 at a cost of $1350. The design shows Gothic influence in its steeply pitched roof, a finial ornament, buttresses, and arched door. Public vaults were used as temporary storage until the cemetery sexton could complete the burial.

Landscape architect John L. Culley was hired to design Lodi's Woodlawn cemetery in 1897. It had decorative iron fencing, two goldfish ponds, "drooping shade trees, and a nicely shaven lawn to greet the eye of the visitor at all times". Eight thousand dollars was allocated by the community for the planning and execution of the cemetery.

Tidy cemeteries and handsome vaults were a source of community pride. The clamor of Litchfield's citizens for a vault resulted in this hewn stone one, built in 1882. It has the entablature and returns of the Greek Revival style, and decorative pinnacles known as *akroterion*.

In 1892, the Medina Women's Cemetery Association raised the funds for this handsome cemetery gate at Spring Grove by selling dinners at the county fair. Stentz and Sheppard of Cleveland were the architects and it was built by Medina's George Gruninger. The main carriage arch and flanking pedestrian entrances are of hewn sandstone with wrought iron gates.

This life-sized sculpture of Cararra marble was originally situated on the Smith homestead in Montville Township. Linus Smith placed the monument on a small rise on the family burial plot in 1879, and added a vault in 1880. Unfortunately, when Linus died, no one was able to locate the vault key, so he was not buried there.

The pioneer figure is a tribute to his father, Fairfax Smith, who settled in Medina County in 1832. The sculpture and pedestal were moved to Spring Grove Cemetery in 1894.

At the end of the Civil War, Medina Company "A" of the Ohio Battalion, National Guard gave eight hundred dollars in company funds to the Medina County Commissioners toward the erection of a Civil War Monument. The Ladies Cemetery association raised another $600, Spring Grove Cemetery donated the lot, and the memorial was finally put up in 1884. It stands on a prominent knoll, visible from Medina Square before the trees along East Liberty Street reached maturity. The full-scale carved stone sculpture has an Eastlake base engraved with the names of Medina soldiers who lost their lives in the War.

The Victorian Era

Our nostalgia for "the good old days" makes us think of sparkling houses set in neat and tidy yards under pollution-free skies. In reality, the landscape was not as a rule attractive or inviting. The trees had all been burnt or exported. Farmyards were workplaces, littered with trash from daily activities. There was too much work to be done to think about pride of place. Village houses fared no better with trash pits and outhouses too close to the homes. Local correspondents in the *Gazette* clamored for neighbors to pull weeds, trim hedges, and pick up litter. Five years after Medina's great fire, the debris still cluttered the sidewalks and roadways.

The industrialization that began to effect metropolitan architecture in the 1830s was evident in Medina County after the Civil War. Machine-made glass and hardware, steam-driven power tools, central heating and standardized paint were available by 1880 and changed the architectural landscape. Housewives who had been reading about efficient kitchens, running water, labor-saving devices, built-in closets, ventilation, and purpose-built rooms in Godey's *Lady's Books* and Catherine Beecher's *American Woman's Home* were now enabled by advances in technology and their husbands' prosperity to have comforts and conveniences hardly dreamed of just a few years earlier. Pioneer women who were bone weary from never-ending tasks now had granddaughters who bemoaned the "servant problem".

Houses could pipe running water via windmills or pumps on an attic or basement cistern. In 1875, the *Gem* building in Wadsworth had "a contrivance for getting up and down stairs". Telephones were available by 1877. Indoor bathrooms were known in the most progressive Medina homes by 1886, although outhouses were common in rural areas until well after the Second World War.

The gas lamps lighting Medina's streets in the 1870s were supplanted by acetylene in the 1880s and "incandescence" in the 1890s. Mud walks were replaced first with boardwalks, then flagstone. The streets around the square were paved with brick in 1894. The invention of the lawnmower replaced the cow and scythe and the American homeowner began to prize large expanses of neatly clipped lawn unknown in other countries. Artificial light and labor-saving inventions made leisure activity possible. By 1877, Medina had a gym, an indoor shooting range, and a tennis club.

Medina's citizens began to prosper when the completion of the canal system fostered the opportunity to market their goods and resources, and the railroad increased these capabilities. Medina County underwent an active building campaign as businessmen and farmers built showplaces to reflect their new and hard-won status. The mortgage system also brought home ownership into the realm of many citizens. There were only twenty-nine mortgages in Medina in 1870, but by 1887 the number had risen to 247 recorded cases.

The invention of the machine-made nail about 1830 allowed for the development of balloon frame construction, a quick and inexpensive framing method utilizing machine-sawn lumber rather than hand-hewn timbers secured with pegs. While finish work continued to be done by hand (as it is today), this labor-saving method allowed homes to be thrown up quickly just as the country was experiencing tremendous growth.

The Victorians were crusaders who sought to reform society. Strict standards were developed for education, morality, propriety, character, and refinement. There was little sympathy for one who veered from the very narrow Victorian path. The American home, too fell within this realm. "Family" and "home" became synonymous as a place where father was king, mother's kindness and wisdom tempered father's rule, and children were clean, starched, and quiet miniature adults. Happy, moral homes made for a happy,

moral society. Interior decoration, home crafts, and decorative arts were layered over every surface to make the home a comfortable haven from the rapidly-changing world. Ladies with time on their hands (the "Devil's workshop") had to keep busy and the invention of mass-produced lithographic printing brought ladies' magazines into middle-class homes. Chairs had throws, doilies, antimacassars, and pillows, generally made by the lady of the house. Pianos had shawls, as no surface could be left bare. Pictures and prints competed for wall space by overlapping one another. House plants and bird cages brought nature indoors.

The love of home and craft extended to the exterior of the house. It was designed and adorned to be warm and welcoming, as well as a work of art reflecting its talented, clever owners.

Large front porches, common by mid-century, extended the living area and added a space for entertaining and leisure activities. The Victorians equated light and air with health and favored lots of large windows, although they covered them under layers of shades, blinds, drapes, shutters, and glass curtains. Coal furnaces put an end to white-painted exteriors, but the development of ready-mixed paints made a wide variety of colors available. Central heating and prosperous times allowed for larger houses. All of these developments led to an architectural period known not by its similarities, but by its variety. The result is a jumble of styles, all collectively known as "Victorian".

After the Civil War, the expanding economy and the growth of both farming and industry created a housing shortage throughout the country. Many new homes were built in Medina County during the last decades of the nineteenth century, and apartment buildings, tenement houses and boarding rooms served many, particularly in the towns and villages. Houses were built as rental properties on speculation, renting for about $100 per year in 1885. Two-family houses were one answer to the need, as they are today. This double house on Vine Street in Medina was photographed in 1910.

"Gingerbread"

During the Victorian Era, the popularity of Gothic novels and nostalgia for picturesque, storybook houses brought about a new style of architecture. People who had grown up with plain, boxy Federal and Greek Revival houses yearned for a style different from that of their parents and grandparents. The availability of steam-powered band saws in Medina about 1880 allowed stern, stark Greek Revival houses to become Victorianized with the addition of a little folk art gingerbread trim. Woodworkers and homeowners could demonstrate their creativity and it is rare to find two houses with exactly the same trim, although this does occur in Marysville. Later trim was scroll-sawn from flat boards, rather than carved three-dimensionally as in the Seymour House of several decades prior. Boards of pine or other soft wood about one and one-half inches thick were pierced, drilled, and sawn into a variety of playful designs. Pendants, vergeboards, finials, gingerbread, decorative brackets and lathe-turned spindles and porch posts earned this style the popular name of "Steamboat" or "Carpenter" Gothic.

Gingerbread, borrowed from the stone crockets, pendants, and finials of Medieval cathedrals covered not only houses, but garden sheds, park shelters, gazebos, burial vaults, and other types of secondary architecture as well as decorative arts (hall trees, hat racks, what-not shelves) that did not even exist in Medieval times.

Delicate detailed trim picked out in a variety of colors required considerable labor to create and maintain. As a result, the trim was often painted all white by the turn of the century when gingerbread curlicues went out of fashion. Succeeding generations viewed the trite Victorian trim with disdain and much of it was removed, but its has enjoyed a revival in recent years.

The Italianate Style

New building was interrupted during the Civil War, and once it began again, no one was interested in the old-fashioned Greek Revival style favored by earlier generations. Builders and homeowners looked to new influences that were the antithesis of the Greek Revival. High ceilings and tall windows, decorative cutwork brackets, bright and varied colors, and taller proportions became popular. The Italianate was the first style to develop wholly in the United States and was referred to in contemporary times as the "American Style". Entrepreneurs and farmers entering the middle class wanted large, substantial houses which reflected their importance and prosperity. New materials, tools, and construction methods were available. Balloon-frame construction, machine-made nails, large panes of plate glass, and machine-planed wood—all known for some time in metropolitan areas—were now available throughout the county. Portable sawmills, available after 1859, were taken from farm to farm to prepare the wood for houses, outbuildings, and barns.

The Greek Revival had been the ubiquitous style throughout the American landscape from about 1830. When its popularity faded, it was not replaced by a single style but rather by a variety of styles all loosely termed "Victorian". The city of Medina, however, is noted for its Italianate buildings. Medina's gradual growth after the Civil War and the 1870 fire in the square meant that many commercial and domestic buildings were erected between 1870 and 1880, the decade of the Italianate Style. Because Medina was not affected by the population growth that much of Northeast Ohio experienced after World War I, its Victorian buildings have not been replaced by subsequent styles.

Though the Italianate style was never known in Italy, its square lines and geometric shapes recalled the Tuscan villas of Northern Italy. The formal symmetry gives it a solid, dignified presence. Notable characteristics include a basic square shape with square or rectangular bays, porches, and additions, a relatively flat roof, a heavy cornice and wide, overhanging eaves often supported with decorative brackets, two-over-two windows, and varied color schemes. Tall ceilings, doors, and windows add to the formality. Industry made possible large panes of glass and scroll saws for decorative brackets and trim and quick construction. Ready-mixed, vibrant colors such as "crushed carrots", "lemon green with bronze trim", "crushed strawberries with mashed tomato trim", and "faded silver with cold gravy" were popular. In 1882, Litchfield Center's Baptist church was painted a "very fashionable crushed green trimmed with dark brown". The invention of Portland cement in 1870 also made brick construction more usual. Brick buildings were trimmed with wooden cornices and brackets which were painted in a variety of hues. Brick storefronts often had cast iron columns and brackets. For the first time, doors were pierced with panes of glass, and double doors were common for houses and shops. Black or American walnut was popular for interior woodwork, although most of the native wood had been destroyed or exported.

Unlike Greek Revival buildings which were low to the ground, Italianate houses and shops are often several steps above ground level to enhance their formality and add a stately approach. The over-all massing is high as well.

Fireplaces are popular once again for nostalgic and aesthetic reasons, though houses were by now heated with furnaces. The resulting chimneys were often designed to reflect the geometric shapes of the house.

Porches were used to emphasize the doorway and add another rectilinear element echoing the body of the building. There were no shutters or blinds to disturb the decorative wooden hood moldings and keystones on the tall, round-headed windows of this South Court Street house.

A reporter for the *Gazette* thought that the new Italianate style of architecture looked like "a cross between a small grain elevator and a country woolen mill". Intensely colored corner boards and trim accentuate the cube-upon-cube massing. This photo of the Reutter homestead in Liverpool Township was taken by photographer E.H. Raber in the 1880s.

Ashabel Holcomb's York Township farmhouse was built in the Italianate style in 1876. The blind window maintains the symmetry of the house.

Albert Munson

The Lyman Munson family was part of the first settlement group in Guilford Township, arriving in 1816. When their daughter died of malaria in that area's lowland, they moved to the hill west of River Styx. There they continued to bear and bury children. Son Albert was one of the few to survive. He grew up on Styx Hill, clerked in the local store and got involved in politics at a very young age. Like H.G. Blake, he "stumped" for his favorite candidates, beginning with presidential candidate John C. Fremont. He also is credited with being the founder of the Republican Party in Medina County. In the course of his politicking, be became a good friend of William McKinley of Canton. He took part in every one of McKinley's campaigns and often served as his nomination orator.

Munson also served in the state legislature but unlike Blake, did not go on to national politics. In 1877, he became Medina County's Probate Judge and moved with his wife and two grown children to their new home on East Washington Street. James G. Hickox built their Italianate house which featured bracketed eaves and a small porch with two front entrances, one leading to the main parlor and the other serving as a "casket door" into the front parlor.

Here the Munsons, a devout family of Spiritualists, regularly held seances and spoke to their dear departed kin. A cousin from River Styx served as the medium for these special evenings. After President McKinley was assassinated, Judge Munson arranged a series of seances in which McKinley talked of his adjustment to the Spirit World and of all the good Republicans in residence there.

Munson was involved in worldly things as well. Before his death, McKinley appointed him postmaster of Medina. He also owned a hardware store with his son Lyman on the south side of Medina square and had an interest in a local stove company. He was clearly a very respected citizen of Medina County, both for his political activities and his business sense.

By 1913, daughter Cora was the last remaining Munson. She ran the family hardware store and lived alone in the house until her death in 1956 at the age of 99. During all those years, she continued to set a place at the table for her parents and her brother, turning their plates over to signify that they were with her in spirit. She left her family home and its contents to the Medina County Historical Society. It served as the local history museum until 1984 when the Community Design Committee, a local preservation group, moved it to Prospect Street and restored it for their offices and a preservation resource center.

The Victorians loved house plants and often had small patches of garden in their yards, but did not favor peripheral planting. Italianate houses, particularly, were raised an elegant distance above ground level in a high foundation, a look which would have been lessened by flowers and hedges.

The Munson house has been relocated to South Prospect Street in Medina and now houses the Community Design Committee offices.

Munson's store still stands on the south side of the square.

One of Medina's finest examples of Italianate architecture has paired decorative brackets supporting a wide overhang, double glazed entry doors, a heavy cornice pierced with oculus windows, and polychrome paint. It was built in 1873 by S.G. Barnard, lawyer, school administrator, and temperance leader.

The Italianate was the first style to employ large panes of window glass and glass panels in the doors, letting light into the front hall. The industrialization of glass production about 1870 made large panes of glass readily available and inexpensive. This house still stands in Lafayette Township and was plaqued as a historic home by the Medina County Historical Society. Mrs. Levie Arnold was the owner in this photograph taken in the 1890s.

Second Empire

The Second Empire period of architecture is named for the distinctive style which originated during the reign of the second French emperor, Napoleon III. In 1829, a large addition with a distinguishing mansard roof was added to the Louvre. Although this was not the first use of windows jutting through an almost vertical roof, the style was universally popular for a short time and is so characterized by its distinctive roofline that it is also known as the mansard style. At this time, France was one of the superpower nations and was the world center of art and fashion, so that the Second Empire style developed there became immensely popular, particularly in the United States which was striving to make itself known internationally. The mansard roof derives its name from that of French architect François Mansart (1598-1666), the premier architect of the French Renaissance period. The Louvre was originally a palace, but was made into a public art gallery in the eighteenth century. Public and government buildings throughout Europe and America followed the example. When Washington, D.C.'s State, War and Navy Building and the Philadelphia City Hall were built in the Second Empire style in 1871, the influence was immediate. The formal design lent itself well to stately, substantial buildings and was heartily adopted for commercial and government buildings and the houses of prosperous merchants and farmers of the new middle class that developed during the Industrial Era.

True Second Empire architecture is fanciful and Baroque, with a profusion of columns, decorative details, molding, repeated motifs, and an eccentric, irregular roofline. On a local level, this has been reduced to a simpler form. The showy and characteristic mansard roofline may be the only decorative element on an otherwise humble building. After the Civil War, architects began to be influenced by the desires of untrained homeowners for the latest styles, however inappropriate. The resulting buildings were often overstated and ungainly, particularly at the close of the Victorian era.

The use of Italianate detailing such as square porches, paired glazed doors, two-over-two sashes, exposed brackets and round-topped windows further dilutes the Second Empire style. As in the Italianate style, brick is often used for Second Empire buildings. The varied hues popular during the 1870s and 1880s are translated into the polychromy of stone trim against brick walls. Wood examples are often painted in a variety of colors for the same effect.

Mansard roofs can be convex, straight, or concave like this example. Patterned slate shingles, brackets, and side and front views of the mansard profile accentuate the prominent roof. Slate was imported from Vermont and Pennsylvania and while it cost about one-third more than wooden shingles, it was free from the problems of freezing, lasted "forever", and made for *cleaner cistern water* in the days when the family's drinking water was collected off of the roof into an underground or basement cistern.

Hiram Bronson walked to Medina from Connecticut in 1818 when he was twelve years old. He later served as sheriff, ran a general store, sat in the Ohio General Assembly, and invested (at great personal loss) in the early railroad system in Medina. He built Medina's best example of the Second Empire/Italianate style in 1873. The bricks were fired at the Sipher and Briggs Brick Company. Architect P.T. Allen of Cleveland designed the house with "invisible" window blinds that tucked into the window jambs, grained woodwork replicating exotic woods, and marble mantles gracing coal-burning fireplaces. With the availability of Franklin stoves in the 1830s, fireplaces were no longer needed, but were included for aesthetic reasons, as they are today.

The tall first-floor windows reflected the eleven foot ceiling heights. The second and ballroom floors had ten-foot ceilings. A decorative iron fence bordered the front yard. Although the Bronson house was one of Medina's finest, it was razed in 1920 when Victorian architecture was considered to be dated and ugly.

Even a small house becomes stately with such an impressive roofline. Large, multiple dormers let light and ventilation into the upper story and offer an additional floor of living space. The square front porch and bay window of this Westfield Township house are borrowed from the Italianate style.

It is said that the mansard or "French" roof became popular in domestic architecture because the owners could gain a floor of space which was not taxed, since taxes were determined by the height to the edge of the roof. This Sharon Center example has a gingerbread porch with turned balusters and porch posts which are atypical for the Second Empire style and probably a later alteration.

Public Buildings

When European settlers first arrived in America, they set aside public lands which belonged to no one person but were open and free to all. That tradition prevailed during the settlement of the Western Reserve, and village squares and town circles are still common throughout the area. In Medina Village, the public square was donated by Elijah Boardman and cleared by Austin Badger in 1818. Central Park in Lodi was "thrown open" as a common ground when the city was established but remained the property of the Harris estate until about 1886. Land was also set aside for government buildings, schools, and cemeteries. The county seat narrowly missed being situated in Weymouth because no one there would donate land for a public courthouse.

In addition to public lands, there are several types of publicly-funded buildings. Schools, hospitals, fire houses, and government buildings such as township, county and village meeting places all have particular space and design needs.

In the early stages of the county's development, specific public meeting places were not a priority. Township and village officers conducted business in homes, churches, or the local general store. However, there was an immediate need for a county courthouse where land deeds could be recorded and court proceedings could be held. Other public buildings were erected later when circumstances and growth in population necessitated them.

Stylistically, public buildings followed the examples set in New England, home of many Medina county settlers. In one parish in Plymouth, Connecticut, 28 of 139 families "joined the trek" to Ohio between 1815 and 1817.

The state legislature created Medina County in 1812 but attached it to Portage County until the Medina population was large enough to hold general elections. In 1818, county officials were in place and the county government began to function. At that point, Medina (then known as Mecca) was but a small clearing in the woods. Rufus Ferris had a double-pen log house on the site of the present Laribee-Hertrick-Bougher law offices on North Broadway. Ferris hosted the first county meeting. The second term was moved to Austin Badger's double log home on the northwest corner of the square. While a traveling judge held court upstairs, the tavern keeper entertained "man and beast" on the first floor.

One of the new county's first official acts was to erect a courthouse. In 1818, carpenter Benjamin Lindsley was contracted to build a two-story brick building with the "inevitable cupola". Lindsley began work immediately, firing the bricks near the village clearing. He ran into financial trouble however, and could not complete the building. The second contract went to John Freese and Timothy Doane. For $1500, Freese and Doane completed the Federal style building with fine details such as flanking stepped gables, double architraves over the front windows, and a second floor courtroom with a brass chandelier. All hardware was hand-wrought of solid brass. Interior doors were black walnut and butternut with hand-forged brass latches. "Wash-board" or wainscoting paneled the first floor rooms. A main entrance in the northwest corner of the building led into an entryway with a staircase. Medina County's citizens took understandable pride in their "pretty, capacious" courthouse in the middle of the Ohio wilderness. It was built on the southwest corner of Liberty and Court streets and gave its name to Court Street, though the current courthouse is now situated on the east side of the square.

Another immediate need was for a jail. The first lock-up was made of logs and was built just south of the courthouse. The cell doors were made of single boards twenty-nine inches wide and two and three-quarters inches thick. The jail was used until 1830 when Sargent and Peak replaced it with a more substantial brick building.

By 1840, the Federal-style courthouse was considered obsolete. The foundation stones from Champion Creek were crumbling and the commissioners feared that the building was unstable. (Apparently they were wrong, since the building still stands.) D.H. Weed received the contract to build a new courthouse on the northeast corner of the square. In return for his work, he received $3100 and the old courthouse building and site. The Weed building was a classic Federal box with a temple front and a cupola. The brick building, trimmed with sandstone sills and lintels, had a "red lead and Spanish brown" interior and sported a flag pole topped with a sixteen-inch gilt wooden ball (now housed at the Medina County Historical Society).

For thirty years this building served the county, but by 1872, more space was needed for county governance. W.G. Tilley built the Second Empire addition which added two large rooms on the first and second floors and adapted the building's design to the new structures going up around the square. A broad flight of stairs and an open portico connected the first floor rooms. On the second level, an open balcony and ornamental belfry completed the design. Records indicate that the total expenditure for the rebuilt courthouse was $23,0365.07. In subsequent years, other additions encased the 1840 building so that the original portion is only discernible through the east facade. A new jail was built adjacent to the courthouse on East Liberty Street.

In addition to administration and legislation, public service was an important function of the government from its inception. Someone had to oversee the poor, attempt to keep the roads and bridges passable, and repair broken fences so that wandering animals could not destroy a farmer's livelihood. Taxes were levied to support institutions for the elderly and infirm. Although it was recognized that not everyone would benefit directly, it was considered "just that they should contribute to the common good". In 1854, the county built its first "poorhouse" on Wedgewood Road in Lafayette Township. This building, put up by William Hickox, burned and was rebuilt in 1864. It grew to be a self-sustaining community with a wash house, bakery, ice house, smokehouse, and coal house. Gardens and orchards supplied much of the food. At one time, the second floor was used as a hospital and the first floor as a home for the insane. The current infirmary was built in 1894.

Medina's citizens were very good to their own. They willingly adopted the orphaned children and rebuilt the burned houses of their friends and neighbors. An outsider, on the other hand, was given a meal and a one-way train ticket "to the place where he was last legally settled".

Soon after settlement, literary societies, lending libraries, and opera houses sprang up in towns and villages throughout the country. The women, especially, appreciated the fact that education and culture were important to the citizens of a community. Seville, Medina, and Lodi were among the towns that had opera houses where popular traveling lecturers and musicians such as the Swedish soprano Jenny Lind would perform. Beginning with Wadsworth in 1822, many towns and churches had a little collection of books that could be borrowed, although a small lending fee was generally charged.

Township and village meeting halls appeared as local communities grew. One of the earliest town halls was in Lafayette. In 1854 the trustees purchased the old Congregational Church and used it for meetings. Wadsworth built its first town hall with council room, post office, municipal court, jail, and a stage for public entertainment in 1867. Litchfield built a brick town hall in 1871, and Seville followed in 1872 with a brick block. It included a community hall where town theatricals and school pageants entertained the citizens. A.M. Williard, the Wellington artist known for *The Spirit of '76*, painted the scenery curtain. This building was lost in a fire in 1964.

Meeting places such as granges and lodges were important to nineteenth century citizens anxious to socialize and exchange ideas with others sharing the same interests.

Although fire was an ever-present hazard in the nineteenth century, few communities had fire-fighting departments. Two major fires in Medina Village caused the residents to build the first "town hall and engine house" in the county in 1878. It was built by Clark and

The Homerville Town Hall in 1908.

Gruninger in the Stick Style. The 28 by 60 foot building has two floors and a bell tower. Two cells kept "vagrants and tramps" from sleeping in the streets. In all $2866 was spent for the lot and building which still stands on the south side of the square.

Medina County also sorely lacked health care facilities well into the twentieth century. Health needs were generally attended to in the home. Extreme cases of illness or injury were sent to Cleveland, although there were stories of appendectomies and tonsillectomies being performed on the kitchen table. Patients with communicable diseases were quarantined in "pest houses" or isolated at home.

Lodi operated a home for mild mental patients in the former home of George W. Jason. It was converted into a hospital in 1920 when a typhoid epidemic struck the town. It was the only hospital in the county until Wadsworth acquired a building from the Ohio Match Company in 1921 and opened a forty-six-bed facility. Medina did not get its first hospital until 1945.

The present Medina County courthouse photographed at the turn of the century. W.G. Tilley's Second Empire addition of 1872 adapted it to the decorative Victorian styles of the buildings which surround the square. Weed's Federal building is barely discernable through the porch columns.

D.H. Weed's 1840 courthouse on the east side of the square as it looked in 1868.

The original courthouse building photographed in the 1960s.

One indication of the prosperity and culture of a community is its generosity in support of public institutions. Medina County built its first facility to care for the elderly poor in 1854. By 1881 the 273- acre county infirmary in Lafayette Township had fifty to sixty patients and cost $4000 annually to maintain and operate. The building was old and unstable, however, and was condemned in 1892. This new infirmary for the care of the elderly was completed in 1894. The second floor and sun porches for "taking the air" were added by the Gruninger Company in 1908. It is still operated by the county as a home for the elderly.

Railroad stations were popular as meeting places just as the general store had been to the preceding generation. Newspapers and magazines were available there, in addition to the latest news from the telegraph wire and from travelers. The first railroad line in Medina County was completed in 1863 in Wadsworth, but the greatest growth was in the 1870s when lines crisscrossed the county and every town clamored for a local station. An 1872 *Gazette* article noted that "the novelty hasn't worn off: crowds still gather at the depot to watch the trains come in". The Stick Style was common because the wide overhangs supported by brackets or kneebraces protected the travelers on the platform. This depot on the Erie Railroad line in Wadsworth was razed in the 1930s.

The Litchfield Town Hall was built by C.P. North and Company in 1871. It was a source of pride for the community and was considered to be "one of the handsomest public buildings in the county". The first floor was used as a select school. Inside, there is a large marble plaque with the names of the Civil War soldiers that Litchfield sent to the War.

The River Styx Town Hall was originally a church building. "Adaptive reuse" has been common throughout the county's history. The church was built in 1851 for the Methodist Episcopal congregation on land donated by early settler David Wilson. The simple frame building, white painted clapboarding, gable roof, and stark design are typical of early church buildings in the county. Only the segmented window over the paneled double doors and a pinwheel roundel decorate this otherwise austere facade.

George Gruninger

George F. Gruninger was born in Liverpool Township in 1850. He learned the trade of carpenter and builder in Akron, coming to Medina in 1870, just after the great fire in the town square. He was a designer as well as a builder. His company was responsible for rebuilding many of the business blocks, including the Renz, Brenner, Griesinger and Asire buildings, and later constructed the *Gazette* Building and the south side of the square to the Phoenix Building. He was also the contractor for St. Paul's Episcopal Church. He erected the Memorial Arch and vault at Spring Grove Cemetery. He built in brick and stone as well as wood, and in several styles, from Italianate to Richardsonian Romanesque. He was responsible for many of the substantial homes on the finest streets in the village.

The plan shown below is of the Liverpool Township School which still exists in Valley City.

Upon his death, the *Gazette* reported that Gruninger "built many business blocks and residences during his long residence here and without a doubt projected his ideas in a physical way onto the community". The fine appearance and condition of these buildings over one hundred years later wonderfully affirms his skill and ability.

Lanterns

Lanterns, also known as belvederes or cupolas, were used to emit light and air into the upper story of a building. They were often built at the top of a staircase so that light could reach to all the floors through the stairwell. The Victorians believed that sunlight provided vitamins which kept one healthy, and that "household murder" was committed by "poisoning and strangulation — the inevitable result of bad air in the private house". As a result, lanterns were advocated by many nineteenth-century writers and by American lecturer Orson Squire Fowler who understood the importance of sunlight and ventilation. He was a proponent of the octagon house, another style which commonly made use of a lantern or cupola.

Lanterns were often used on Tuscan architecture which was influenced by the flat, square villas of the Italian countryside. In addition, they can be added to any flat-roofed type of architecture, such as the Italianate or the hip-roofed version of the Greek Revival style.

The Zimri Cook house in Lester is one of Medina County's finest homes. Cook came to Medina from Jefferson County, New York in 1813 with his parents and nine siblings (whose names all began with the letter "Z".) He built this fine hip-roofed Greek Revival with a center lantern in 1846 at a taxable value of $322. There is an entablature around the main body of the house, the ell, and the lantern. The corner pilasters extend through both floors of the house. The doorway, with Doric columns and sidelights, has the original door, hardware, and glass. The house is listed on the National Register of Historic Places.

Alexander Whiteside, leading Seville citizen, auditor, and commissioner built this house about 1855. Guilford Township had one of the earliest brick kilns in the area, established about 1823 by Henry Hosmer. This house is only one of three Medina County buildings listed on the Historic American Building Survey conducted by the Federal government in 1934 when architects traveled throughout the country documenting fine examples of early architecture. This detail drawing shows the frieze band of the Whiteside house decorated with hand-carved metopes and triglyphs, the only one of its type in the county.

Old Ladies' Home ~ -LODI O.-

In 1895, Mrs. Elvira Ainsworth and Mrs. Clarissa Rounds established the Home for Aged Women of Medina County, Ohio. The "Ainsworth Lodge", as it was known, was located in Lodi and endowed with $20,000 and the rental income from the J.W. Wolcott block. The house that they purchased from the Alexander Whiteside estate was an Italianate with square cupola, floor–to-ceiling first story windows, and a five-bay porch. The chimneys are placed as far to the rear of the house as possible, since chimneys were not found on houses in Italy.

Many lanterns, perched at a steep and hard-to-reach place, were removed or lost to neglect over subsequent years.

Smith Southard Hospital Lodi Ohio.

The Italianate home of George W. Jason was built in Lodi in the 1860s. He was a wholesale and retail dealer in "pianofortes, organs, and melodeans". His large house had an octagonal tower with decorative brackets supporting the overhang, a wide frieze band, and round-topped windows matching those of the house. Jason had a deer park on his property. In 1874 he paid $300 for two antelopes imported from Kansas. The animals were always breaking loose, however, and were considered a nuisance by the community. The house became the Smith Southard Hospital, forerunner of the Lodi Community Hospital, after Jason's death in the 1890s.

The Edward Talbot house just south of Chatham Center is referred to as "Tuscan Italianate" by the historic buildings inventory conducted on Medina County architecture in 1979. The house, built in 1860, has standing seam metal roofing, very tall two-over-two sash windows, decorative brackets supporting the full-facade porch, and round-topped windows in the lantern. Exposed rafters, echoed by decorative brackets, support the wide overhangs of the main body of the house and of the lantern.

Stick Style

During the second half of the nineteenth century, a variety of styles, all loosely termed "Victorian", were utilized. Advances in technology, communications, and transportation meant that there was no longer a delay between metropolitan and provincial building styles. One Victorian style, known as "Stick", was common throughout the United States after about 1875. It is considered by many to be a derivative of the Gothic Revival style, as evidenced by the decorative work in the gables, but there is an emphasis on the surface texture not found in Gothic Revival buildings.

The distinguishing characteristic is the decorative surface pattern created by placing the siding in a variety of directions. The universal adoption of industrialized housing construction after the Civil War left some yearning for the craftsmanship of traditional handbuilding skills. This style sought to emphasize the framing and to "honestly" reflect the support structure beneath the decorative surface. The siding or clapboarding can be laid in a combination of vertical, horizontal, or diagonal patterns. This use of thin "stick" trimming and bracing and a surface pattern reflective of the building's framework are typical of the Stick Style.

Notable characteristics are asymmetry, steep roofs, first- and second-story porches, bay windows, exposed eave and porch rafters, and diagonal braces. Narrow clapboards accentuate the decorative surface pattern. There is often trusswork or stickwork in the gable, representative of the supportive trusswork, but merely decorative. Since Stick architecture can be adorned with Eastlake, Classical, or other motifs, it is actually a design of form rather than a surface style.

O.C. Shepard owned the feed store and mill in Medina. He sold seventy-five bushels of flour a day under his private brands "The Magnificent", "The Splendid", and "Grandfather's Whole Wheat". His Stick Style house was built by J.W. Martin. The 32 by 44 foot house had nine rooms and cost $2200 to build in 1884. The porch with short posts on cast concrete pedestals is a twentieth-century modernization.

Medina boot and shoe dealer C.L. Griesinger hired the Gruninger Brothers to build his Stick Style house from May to December, 1886, and is notable for its irregular, picturesque silhouette, as though its form had developed over the years like a Medieval cottage. Balloon framing allowed for small extensions, rooms jutting at angles from the main body of the house, multiple corners, and a hexagon-shaped dining room. The "colored glass" windows were designed by Barge and Gross. The interior had red oak, chestnut and cherry woodwork. The bedrooms were connected by portieres (doorways hung with heavy curtains), and the parlor, dining room, and bedroom were heated by grates (coal-burning fireplaces).

C.M. Spitzer's "sumptuous mansion" was built in Medina Village in 1890. The decorative stickwork indicating the underlying framework and fishscale clapboards make it a Stick Style house, although it was called "German Renaissance" in its day. It had bath and toilet rooms, "imitation" fireplaces, beveled glass entry doors, and was lighted and heated by a gas machine in the cellar.

The Spitzer carriage house was designed to match the main house and has identical trusswork, fishscale roofing slates, multiple gables, and shaped clapboard siding. The louvered lantern or cupola ventilated the hayloft. The building is now a private residence.

The old Newton homestead in Homerville was built in about 1880. The projecting gable, diagonal and horizontal studs in the gable trusswork, patterned slate roof tiles and pendants dripping from the lacey gingerbread trim are characteristics of the Stick Style of architecture.

Wadsworth Township's Wall house was built by a successful farmer in about 1880. The brick house has Stickwork trim in the gable, a shallow truncated hip roof with ornamental iron cresting, round-topped windows from the Italianate style, and a row of blind windows. Rick-rack trim adorns the wide frieze band.

Ephriam Hunsberger built this house in 1883. He and his brother Christian owned a Wadsworth blind, door and sash factory. In 1864, Hunsberger donated the land for the Wadsworth Mennonite College building. From 1896 to 1950, members of the Wertz family lived here. Lloyd S. Wertz owned the Wertz Buggy Company with his brother C.B. and was Wadsworth mayor from 1889 to 1905.

Typical Stick Style characteristics on this Medina house are gable trusswork, thin clapboards laid in a variety of directions, hexagonal fishscale slate roofing shingles, and a square turret or tower. Square towers are more typical on Stick Style houses than on Queen Anne buildings.

Nelson Waltz was a builder who worked for Medina's Bennet Lumber Company, still in operation. He built his Stick Style home on West Washington Street in 1890. The second floor sleeping porch was a popular feature on houses built during the years when tuberculosis and influenza were common. The photograph was taken in 1977.

Eastlake

After the Civil War, the United States grew in unprecedented numbers. Immigration, westward expansion and the development of a large middle class meant that hundreds and thousands of new homes were built and furnished during the last decades of the century.

A new style of architecture, named for the man who influenced it, became very popular during the Victorian era. British author and designer Charles Locke Eastlake lamented the fact that Americans were ingenious in inventing new machinery and techniques for building, yet built in traditional, derivative styles of other countries and eras. He thought that we should develop a new decorative vocabulary which lent itself to machine-made products. Corruptions of his designs were applied to a variety of building components: porch trim, window and door surrounds, brackets, and brickwork. A reaction against the heavy, neo-Rococo mid-century furniture, Eastlake decoration is symmetrical and flat, with shallow foliate and geometric designs produced by machine—pierced or cut with a scroll saw—not hand carved. His book *Hints on Household Taste* was published in the United States in 1872 and was immensely popular here. The Eastlake style decorated everything from buildings to umbrellas from about 1875 to 1890. Many of the Stick and Queen Anne buildings erected during this time employ Eastlake decorative trim.

Characteristics of the Eastlake house are steep gable roofs, first and second-story porches with lathe-turned spindles and posts, and trademark pierced decorations. An asymmetrical, irregular shape, as though the house had been altered and added to over the years, was attractive to people who were weary of the machine-built order and symmetry of the Second Empire and Italianate styles of architecture.

Dr. W.B. Croft, a popular Medina surgeon, was a proud graduate of the Cleveland Homeopathic Hospital College, one of the finest and most progressive in the country. He built this spacious Eastlake style house on West Liberty Street in 1886. The large front porch offers protection from heat and storms and privacy for the occupants. The square tower has a wide frieze band with shallow machine-cut Eastlake decorations. The second-story porch, multiple roof shapes and levels, stained glass windows and ridgetop embellishments are all typical of the style.

Nelson Burnham's house has a Queen Anne silhouette and square and conical towers, Eastlake pierced decoration, and a stone stringcourse adding interest to the brick walls. The Stick Style truss work and deep overhangs supported by large knee braces add a three-dimensional quality. Gables, dormers, and towers each have their own roof, adding to the picturesque quality. The fourteen-room mansion has four floors, with a ballroom on the third floor. Carpenters worked on the inside carving and staining the wood for over a year. The "metropolitan like" house was built by Burnham, a wealthy farmer, in 1880 for his daughter Nell as part of her inheritance. It still stands in Medina.

Paul C. Parker was a Medina millwright and bridge builder. He built his Eastlake style house in 1883 for about $3000. Complex, three-dimensional brickwork lends a sculptural, robust quality to the chimney, centrally positioned and inlaid with a terra cotta medallion for emphasis.

While hauling paving stones for the cellar, Parker tripped and one of the large pavers fell on him. He lingered for several days, but finally died of internal injuries.

John Smart immigrated to Medina from New York. He helped to found the Hollow Ware factory in Medina and in 1886 built his showplace home on North Elmwood Street. The Smart family lived here until the turn of the century, and their two daughters were married in the front parlor. Subsequent owners were the Baldwin family, owners of the *Gazette*, and the William Hammerschmidts who operated a large greenhouse. The Eastlake style house has a square conical tower, several porches, pierced Eastlake-decorated trim, and stained glass windows. It has been the home of the Medina County Historical Society since 1984.

The W.H. Albro home was designed by Michigan architect D.P. Clark and built by Charles Heacox in 1886. It had "colored glass windows", a red oak interior, bay windows, a soapstone kitchen sink, a force pump to a cellar cistern supplying water to the entire house, a covered passageway to the wood and coal house, interior window blinds imported from Michigan, a four inch thick concrete basement floor and a total cost of over $4000. Yet the *Gazette* considered this to be "elegant, comfortable, and not expensive", although the average house cost was about $700 at this time. Bedroom colors were cherry, blue, and peach blow; there were closets in each bedroom and one for fur storage. All hardware was solid brass. This "ornament to the village" was burglarized and vandalized by someone who put "raspberries and cheese in the commode". After a second incident, a robber wearing "pointed dude shoes" was apprehended. A wire alarm system was added in 1896.

Queen Anne

Just as the Victorian interior was a miscellany of patterns, shapes, textures, and colors, the exterior was punctuated with a variety of towers, bay windows, porches, balconies, and additions. These exterior shapes reflected the new use of space inside. Room size, shape, and even floor levels varied in response to new uses. Whereas the timber-framed Federal or Greek Revival house had a symmetrical floor plan continued unchanged over the centuries without regard to convenience or use, the Queen Anne house was designed to be functional. New rooms—pantries, sewing rooms, dressing rooms, studies, sleeping porches, sun rooms—were developed in response to the needs and activities of smaller but more prosperous families. The rising importance of children in the family led to individual bed/playrooms for each child. The electrification of homes (in Medina County beginning about 1890) also allowed for separate, disparate rooms designed for varied uses. The availability of electricity and central heating resulted in large houses, generally two stories and an attic. Kitchens were no longer the main activity (and warmest) room in the house, and were reduced in size accordingly. Dining rooms were a reflection of the gathering together of the family members for shared activities. The parlor, that rarely-used room to which earlier families had devoted precious space and money, began to be abandoned in favor of more space for the family. By 1890, fewer than half of the floor plans included parlors.

The Queen Anne style was originated and named by the English architect Richard Norman Shaw. It has nothing to do with the eighteenth-century queen or her era, but uses the steep gable roofs, irregular shapes, and organic materials of Medieval English styles. It was primarily a domestic architecture: picturesque, bulky, asymmetrical, and homey. Stone, earthy colors, patterned shingles and wood siding bind the house to its setting and present a welcoming facade.

Asymmetrical verandahs are supported by balusters and posts made of turned spindles. This delineates the porch as an outdoor room and a private space rather than simply an element drawing the eye to the facade. The front doorway, lost in the shadows of the deep porch, is not an important design element of the Queen Anne house.

In the previous decade, the Italianate style projected the authoritative image that reflected the owner's position. Now, rambling "cottages" turned their emphasis to the family's needs. Queen Anne houses have open floor plans with rooms flowing into one another. Hardwood paneling, built-in window seats, benches, and bookcases made with beautifully grained woods integrate the spaces.

Fancy, finicky designs tend to fade from popular favor quickly. The style lasted only for about twenty years before homeowners were attracted to newer types of architecture, but the Queen Anne and its variant styles were extremely popular during the last decades of the nineteenth century.

The Queen Anne house often is based upon a hip-roofed square with added dormers, porches, and bay windows. The entry porch extending from the corner of this Westfield Center house is a typical element on this type of Queen Anne building. The truncated hip roof, having the corner peak sheared off, is also common.

A small, squat, conical turret, large wrap-around verandah, second story porch, Ionic columns, and stained glass windows are typical Queen Anne elements of this house in Seville.

W.H. Sipher was born in Germany and emigrated to Medina in 1849. He was part-owner of the Sipher and Briggs brickyard which he founded in 1873 on the banks of Champion Creek. His brick Victorian house with ten rooms and a garret was put up in 1885, with a large extension added in 1890.

G.W. Reinhardt's East Washington Street house in Medina was built in 1885-86. Reinhardt, who owned a Medina bakery and restaurant, stocked "leading brands of canned goods, confectionery, ice cream, soda water, fruit in season, in fact, everything that is handled by a first class baker". The house was built by George Gruninger. The selection of the Queen Anne style indicated Reinhardt's status as a successful entrepreneur in town.

The H.E. Matteson house in Seville was built by a local merchant in 1888. Elements from the Stick Style are the square tower, fishscale siding, and sawtooth trim. Several blind windows in the tower add aesthetics rather than light and air. This house has been adapted for use as a funeral home.

Albert Nettleton's Queen Anne style house on East Washington Street in Medina was built about 1883. The octagonal turret or tower and large verandah are typical of the style. The house is basically a hip-roofed square with a variety of gable peaks adding interest to the surface.

Lost towns, forgotten places

Early Medina County maps indicate many place names that have long been forgotten. They are crossings or small clusters of buildings which at one time had a name and often a post office. When two roads intersected, the locals liked to name the site. Thus the old maps abound with names like Young's Corners, Fixler's Corners, or Remsen Corners, named after a prominent landowner in the area.

In other cases, communities, as we know them today, went through many name changes. Medina was originally named Mecca until 1819 when the Federal postmaster discovered that there was a Mecca in Trumball County. To facilitate mail delivery, they changed the name from Mohammed's birthplace to his final resting place and the name of the county. Sharon Center was initially Hart and Mather after the township's principle owners. It became Gask for Peter Moore's beloved Scottish birthplace and finally Sharon after the Connecticut hometown of another settler. In 1828, the Federal post office forced Wilson's Corners in Guilford Township to change its name, so River Styx was selected after the Biblical dismal swamp. Harrisville Center was renamed Harrisville Reserve and finally Lodi for an important battle in the Napoleanic Wars, and Liverpool Center became Valley City in 1910. Whittesley is now known as Lafayette.

Sharon Township had a number of interesting hamlets. One that barely remains is Windfall, on the top of the hill on Route 18. When the settlers first arrived in that area, they found that huge trees had been felled by a storm, a windfall of fuel and building materials. West of Sharon on Sharon-Copley Road is Boneta, named for the niece of Abraham Shontz. To the locals, it was known as "Stingy Man's Crossing" because Shontz chased away the school children who stopped at his pond for water. At the crossing of Beach and Fixler Roads was Katytown, probably named after the Kate who ran the general store in the area.

Other location names reflected their geographical situation. In the northeastern part of the county, noted for its hills and hollows, there is Hinckley Ridge, a distinctive section of Hinckley Township east of the center. The name never appeared on maps, but it was certainly imbedded in the hearts of the people who grew up there. In Granger Township, the history books speak of Potter's Pinnacle. The name and location have disappeared, but there are many nineteenth-century references to it. "Bogus Hollow", west of Litchfield Center, described an incident in which molding dies for minting counterfeit coins were found.

A number of small towns and crossroads villages sported a general store and post office in the days before the automobile. A post office called Haldo opened to serve the huge farms at Lodi. In 1890, the tiny hamlet of Pawnee in Chatham Township changed the name of its post office to Munson in honor of the Medina judge. Once rural delivery was available, the post offices were closed, the general store faded away, and many towns disappeared. Esselburn's Corners was a small village located three miles west of Lodi. It was settled by German immigrants and the Esselburn family operated a general store and post office there.

Westfield Township was named after the Massachusetts home town of part owner Samuel Fowler. Friendsville was a village that grew up west of the Westfield Center. It was noted for its Quaker or "Friends" population and had the township post office before it was moved to LeRoy. The name LeRoy originally came from the local post master. When the Ohio Farmers' Insurance Company changed its name to Westfield Insurance, the village renamed itself after its largest employer.

Marysville, in the northern part of Liverpool Township, was first known as Salt Spring Town and later named in honor of the wife of landowner H.H. Coit. It first appeared that the area would flourish. Early maps show platted streets in neat little rectangles in anticipation of the growth of the community. The locals changed the name to Hardscrabble when land could not be sold after the salt mines gave out. Like other villages, the railroads passed them by, the post office closed, and the town faded from memory.

Risley, in Litchfield Township, developed on the Pennsylvania and Western railroad line. It was supposedly named after the first passenger who alit there. The first building was a combination house/general store/post office/barber shop. Other buildings soon sprang up to serve the passengers. In 1905, sparks from the train ignited the store and another house. The train which had brought Risley to life destroyed it within just a few years, although it remains on some maps.

Western Star and nearby Wadsworth were both pleasant villages with growing populations and centers of commerce in the nineteenth century, but Wadsworth was given an impetus for growth when the railroad situated a depot there; Western Star all but disappeared from the map as a separate village.

In Hinckley, the area of Whistle Alley was named for a family in the area who liked to whistle. Egypt, Worden, Chamberlain, Paxton, and Council Corners have all vanished as communities, but still appear on some area maps and in the recollections of some local citizens.

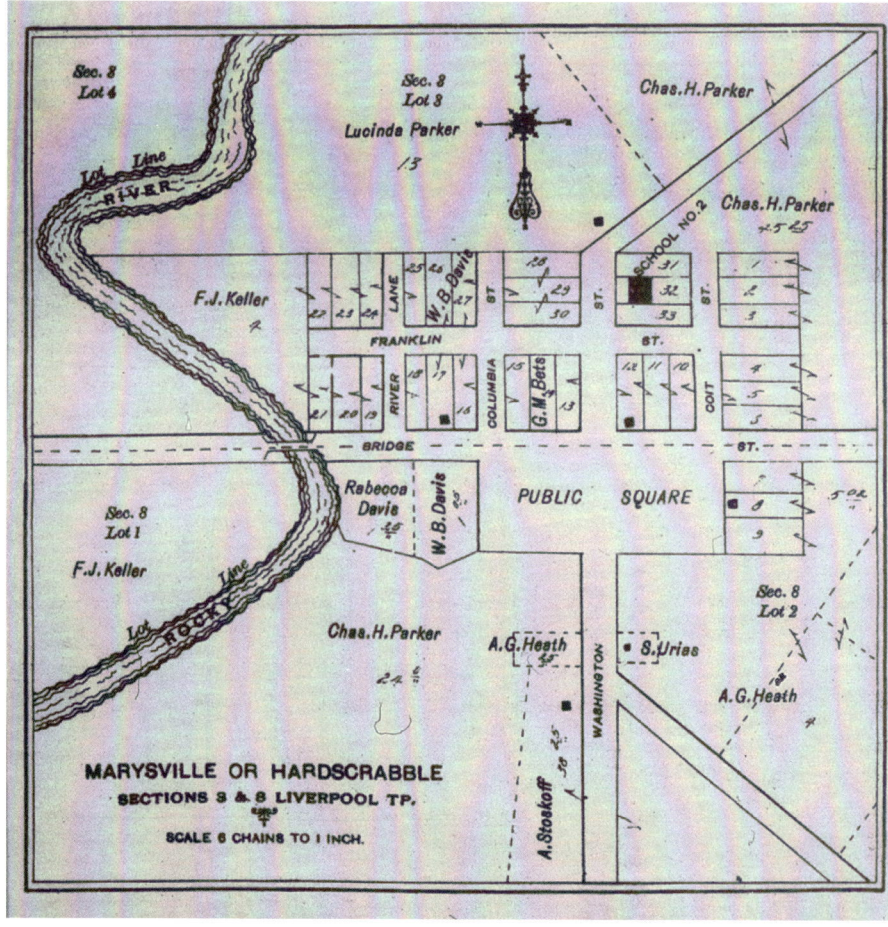

A plat map of Marysville or Hardscrabble in Liverpool Township from the 1897 Medina County atlas. The village was divided into residential lots with provisions for a town square, streets, and a schoolhouse (which still stands) in anticipation of the growth of the town.

Shingle Style

One of the styles that was a sub-set of the Queen Anne is known as the "Shingle Style", named for its materials. Houses sided with wooden shingles had been built along the Atlantic coast from earliest settlement times, and nineteenth-century architects such as Henry Hobson Richardson adopted the material for summer houses there. These houses were well received and influenced the comfortable, domestic architectural style popular throughout the 1880s. It was a machine-built form taking full advantage of contemporary tools and building techniques, but seeking to reflect nature in its appearance and materials. The profile of the house is often reduced to one large, encompassing dormer, as though the house had grown out of the earth. Organic materials and colors furthered this appearance.

The burgeoning economy of the 1880s expanded job opportunities and caused tremendous growth, but also made people nostalgic for earlier, pre-industrial times. Now that Medina County had burned and exported all of its hardwood forests, wood was again appreciated. Fifty thousand board feet of walnut was exported from Homerville in 1870 alone. A farmer related in 1873 that he had burned acres and acres of hardwood while settling his farm in the 1830s, and now had to buy wood imported from Michigan to build and roof a barn. The warmth and beauty of wood was once again desired. Wood shingles sheath the walls. The wood shingle roof sweeps down to encompass the first story, and often has a large dormer—the size of an entire room—poking through it. Inside, woodwork made of fine woods was stained to enhance the natural grain. Soft woods were grained in imitation of oak, chestnut, cherry, or other decorative woods. Flowery, patterned carpets were replaced with inlaid wood floors.

The Shingle Style, with its emphasis on natural materials, quality workmanship, and the honest exterior form which followed interior functions, influenced twentieth-century architects, particularly Frank Lloyd Wright. By the 1880s the common woods were pine and whitewood, which had to be stained or painted to protect them from the elements, but earth-toned hues such as gray, green, brown, and ochre were used. Shallow eaves and a horizontal, ground-hugging design draw the house down to the earth. Some examples have Queen Anne towers, but they are squat so as not to distract from the low-lying effect. Porches are "carved out" from the body of the house. Overhangs are very shallow so that the textured wall surface is not hidden in shadows. The silhouette is irregular and asymmetrical as though the house grew and expanded over the years.

The Shingle Style was popular in the United States throughout the 1880s and 1890s but there are few Medina County examples, compared to the Eastlake, Stick, and Queen Anne styles favored here. The few that were built, however, are fine examples of their type.

Small-paned windows with lozenge-shaped lights and a narrow overhang or eave are common features of the style. Emphasis is on the wall surface rather than decorative trim.

This Wadsworth house has a long, sloping roofline, oculus windows, a second-story balcony, and an oriel window. Yellow glazed brick, slate roof tiles, and earth-toned stains nestle the house close to its setting. The conical towers are lower than those of the Queen Anne period, keeping the overall massing low to the ground.

M iss Effie Babcock built a 25-room "addition" onto her Sharon Center house in 1897. The Shingle Style house has two towers, decorative chimneys, second story porches, a Dutch gambrel roof, and a balustered porch. Wooden shingles cover the roof and wall surfaces. The porte-cochere protected the family from the weather as they alit from their carriages. For a time, the house was used as a tuberculosis sanitarium. In 1931 it burned, and the loss was valued at $25,000.

E .B. Brenner owned a hotel and apartment buildings in Medina Village. His Shingle Style house was built in 1888 for $1020. The huge dormer with its little balcony window, sweeping roofline, and shingle roof and siding are hallmarks of the style. Narrow overhangs do not detract from the patterned siding.

McDowell House

Banker, druggist, cheese maker, Civil War veteran—all of these roles shaped R. M. McDowell and made him a prosperous leading citizen of Medina. Such a position required a substantial house for entertaining and for raising a large family. In 1890, McDowell contracted with architect George Nettleton of Detroit and moved an ante-bellum house from his lot at the end of West Washington Street in preparation for his new house. From that vantage point, his impressive home would be imposing indeed as it looked down one of Medina's finest streets toward town center and his Old Phoenix Bank. McDowell chose the Shingle Style for his large, rambling house which epitomized the exuberance of the Victorian Era.

McDowell spent $10,800 on "the Big House" at a time when a three bedroom house with a "proper basement cistern" cost less than $1000. Seven employees of Medina's Gruninger Brothers building company worked nine hours a day, six days a week at $13 per week on the house. In 1892, it was completed with seven fireplaces, an attic cistern for gravity-fed plumbing to the bathrooms, a basement chemical plant that produced gas for lighting, and a dumb-waiter to carry wood to the fireplace—all of the most modern conveniences.

The house has all of the hallmarks of the Shingle Style. The complex exterior is embellished with balconies, stained glass windows, a projecting tower, bays, a large wrap-around porch, and a porte cochere. The massing is irregular, reflecting the varied room uses. Various geometrical shapes create an asymmetrical roofline and add to the picturesque quality. Stone, clapboard, and wood shingles texture the surface. There are many Classical details—a Palladian window, tiny window panes, steep gable roofs, paired and grouped windows, wooden shingles like the early Dutch settlement houses— so many that a contemporary *Gazette* account called it "Colonial Style".

The family still owns the house today, four generations after McDowell built it.

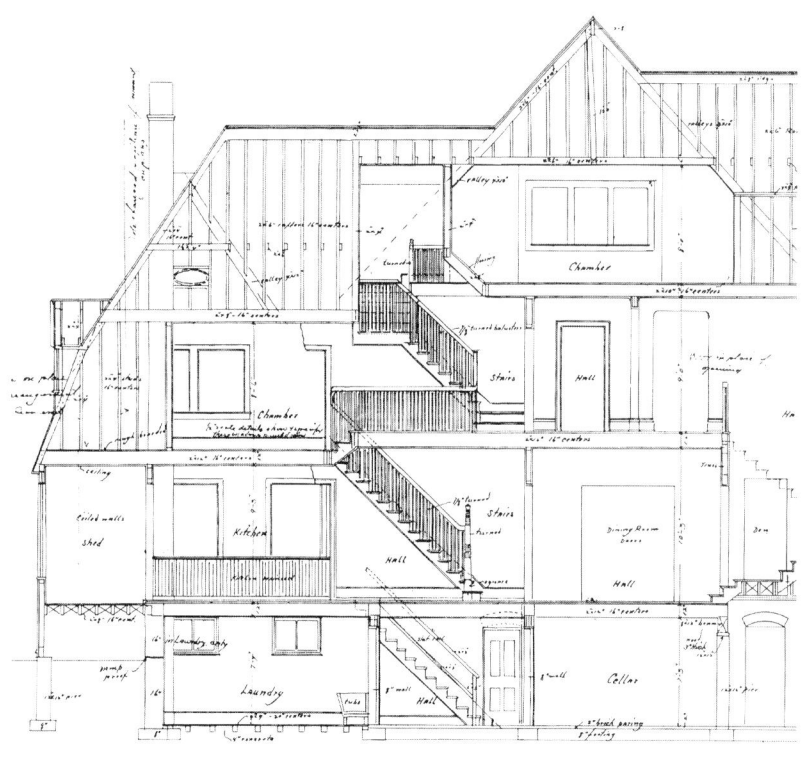

R.M. McDowell and his brother, O.H. moved into identical Italianate houses at the end of West Washington Street after they were married to H.G. Blake's two daughters in 1876. R.M. was never pleased with his house, however, and built this impressive home across the street where he could view the sleighs and horses that often raced up and down West Washington Street.

People

Many noteworthy men and women contributed to the history of Medina County throughout its formative years.

Harrison G. Blake was one of the county's leading historic figures. He overcame early hardships to become a merchant, banker, newspaper editor and Unites States Representative. His remarkable story began in Vermont in 1821. Blake was an infant when his parents were caught in a snow storm. They became stranded in deep snow, and Blake's father set off on foot to seek help. Mrs. Blake stayed behind, wrapping her baby in her cloak. Sometime later rescuers found the father, semi-conscious, only a hundred yards from his wife and baby. He weakly held up two fingers to indicate their presence. When they found Mrs. Blake she was barely alive. Both parents soon died and baby Harrison was left an orphan.

A family friend, Jesse Rhoades, took in the baby. Blake was nine when the Rhoades family moved to Guilford Township in 1830. At sixteen, he came to Medina and clerked in a local store while reading for the bar under Judge J.S. Carpenter. By 1859, he owned the store and practiced law with the firm of Blake and Woodward. His next venture was banking. He organized the Phoenix Bank, first as a private institution and later as a national bank. During this time, he was also editor of the *Gazette*, which gave him the most influential voice in town.

Blake served in the Civil War in Virginia as Colonel in the 166th

Regiment of the Ohio National Guard. Upon his return to Ohio, he became interested in politics. He "stumped" for Benjamin Harrison, traveling throughout the county, speaking from the tops of stumps to anyone who would listen. He earned a reputation as a fine orator, a roll he was called upon to fill at many Medina events. In 1846, at age 25, he was elected to the lower house of the state legislature and became speaker of the Ohio Senate. Blake served two terms in the United States Congress, beginning in 1858. It is said that he befriended President Lincoln during his first administration because they had both lost young sons. Together, they walked the gardens of the White House and talked of their boys. Blake's lasting legacy on the national level was the creation of the money order system.

One of Medina's first settlers, Charles Olcutt, was born in Manchester, Connecticut in 1793. He studied law at Yale and was a scientist and inventor who designed the first ironclad warship. He came to Medina in 1818 and practiced law. He was quite successful, serving as Medina County Prosecutor from 1825 to 1830.

In 1834, a stage traveling from Columbus to Cleveland stopped in Seville for a fresh team. Two horsemen followed the coach, which carried two Indian men and two slave girls. The men had been attending a select school at Great Crossing, Kentucky. There, they were guests of Colonel Richard M. Johnson and met and fell in love with the slave girls, one of whom was Johnson's daughter. The four contrived a plan to escape north to freedom in Canada.

After their capture in Seville, they were brought before Austin Wilder, the Medina Township Justice of the Peace holding jurisdiction under the fugitive slave law. Charles Olcutt defended the slaves, but they were returned to Kentucky and to slavery. No criminal charges were brought against the men. Johnson went on to become Vice President under Martin Van Buren.

Olcutt remained in Medina and grew more eccentric as the years progressed. His anti-slavery treatise "proved" for three hundred pages that Christ was an abolitionist. He was "filthy to an unspeakable degree'" and lived in a tiny room near the door of the courthouse. He escaped the fire of 1848 with only two iron ship models and a pair of pants. After the fire, he lived off the kindness of his neighbors and died in the county infirmary in 1857, a "poor old wise simpleton" who was rightly convinced that his iron ship would one day be adapted for all oceanic navigation.

Austin Gray Cherry, the editor of the *Young Folks' Gem*, emigrated to Sharon from New Jersey in 1856. Some time after his settlement, he learned that he was heir to an English earldom and left for England. He got as far as New York but returned to Sharon to his "demented wife and crippled child". The child was P.P. Cherry who went on to write several historical books of great local interest. P.P. worked in Akron's B.F. Goodrich plant when it had only thirty employees. He died at age eighty-eight in 1937 and is buried in God's Acre at Sharon Center.

For people born in the 1820s, life expectancy was less than 42 years. Lodi's Chedon Lomer Griffin was famous for his great age. He remembered his brother going off to the Revolutionary War and cast his first presidential ballot for John Adams. He claimed to have been born in 1760 and was an eccentric who received much press in the United States and his native England during the last several years of his life. He was quite often visited by sightseers—whom he charged a two dollar fee—and news journalists. After his death in 1878, his true age was established as 106; he had been the oldest living American.

He outlived two wives and his third had a baby while he was already quite elderly. He lost an arm when a tree limb fell on it. Thinking that he was near death, his wife promised to name the baby after him. "No", he said, raising his head, "name the next one after me."

Hiram Miller escorted and sheltered two hundred runaway slaves. He was physically abused for his acts and endured much ridicule and harassment. His own church rejected him, but he returned, with a slave friend. They were denied a seat but sat on the wood pile next to the stove, letting the logs roll noisily to remind the congregation of their presence. Miller was ostracized by his neighbors and under the Fugitive Slave Act, placed himself at risk of losing all of his assets. A plaque honoring Miller stands near his tiny house in Hinckley Township.

Gertie Lewis does not fit the picture of a sheltered Victorian lady. She attended Buchtel College in 1888 and had a successful career as an artist. As the daughter of a wealthy Medina judge and according to the conventions of the day, she would not have worked, but she supported herself by exhibiting and selling her drawings and paintings and operated teaching studios in Akron and Cleveland. For a time, she painted china for a Barberton company. She continued to educate herself traveling throughout the country to study. She was engaged to be married but broke off the engagement because, according to the *Gazette,* he was not equal to her station. He asked to meet with her and when she arrived at his house, he tried to kill her. She was saved by the mailman who heard the commotion. She married at the age of thirty-one, "using the ring service and omitting the religious part."

Hinckley native Amos Webber was a lawyer who later settled in Lorain. He served as trustee and historian of Baldwin-Wallace College, was Lorain County prosecutor and common pleas judge, and president of the Anti-saloon League. As United States Congressman, he introduced the first Prohibition legislation and organized a two thousand member march on Washington, D.C. His autobiography and history of Hinckley are valuable resources for the study of local history.

Cattle dealer Robert Whipp emigrated from England when he lost his entire stock to disease. He came to Hinckley to start over and made his fortune in the inflated beef prices during the Civil War. He built, little by little, a 3000-acre estate by taking over farms, but allowed them to decay and livestock to wander through the houses. His second wife convinced her lover and her brother to try to kill him for his $100,000 estate after one week of marriage and she was sent to the state penitentiary. He was blind and desolate at the end of his life and after his death in 1890 his property was sold to settle his taxes and repay his debts.

"Uncle" Thomas Easton was a farm laborer who never earned more than a dollar a day in his life yet amassed a $30,000 fortune. He saved bits of scrap iron and rags to sell. When farmers cleared acreage, he sold the treetops for firewood. He paid for all his goods in labor. He read by the light of the stove fired with shavings from the hollow ware factory. He bought bonds and securities with his pinched pennies and of his fortune he gave $18,000 toward the education of poor students at Baldwin (now Baldwin-Wallace) College.

Russell Alger was born in Whittesley, Lafayette in 1836. As a young man, he supported himself as a farm laborer earning $3 a month and board. He was self-educated and admitted to the bar in 1859. After serving in the Civil War, he became governor of Michigan, then United States Senator, and was later made Secretary of War under President McKinley.

Captain Martin Van Buren Bates and his wife, Anna Swan, were truly giants in their day. Bates, born in Kentucky in 1845, grew to seven feet, eight inches and weighed 480 pounds. Anna Swan, from Nova Scotia, was seven feet, eleven inches tall and weighed over four hundred pounds. Captain Bates was the last of eleven children and the only one to reach such extraordinary height. As a young man, he joined the Rebel forces fighting in the hills around his home. Apparently, he was elected captain by his unit but saw little action in battle. He was captured early in the War and spent most of the time as a prisoner in Columbus where he was exhibited as "The Largest Rebel Ever Caught". After the War, he returned to Kentucky to find his homestead burned and the family scattered, so he wandered back north to Cincinnati. There he signed on with Judge Ingall's show of human oddities that was preparing to travel throughout Europe.

Anna Swan grew up in Nova Scotia. She was the third of thirteen children and weighed eighteen pounds at birth. By age four, she reached over five feet and could already look her mother in the eye. By her teens, she was over seven feet tall. In spite of her abnormal size, she dreamed of becoming a teacher and for a time attended a normal school. She took up three beds and had to do all of her

schoolwork seated on the floor. Soon the distraction of her oddity caused the school administration to ask her to withdraw. She joined P.T. Barnum's museum and menagerie in New York City and then Ingall's tour of Europe.

Captain Bates and Anna Swan met on board ship, decided that they were made for each other, and were engaged by the time they landed. While visiting the courts of England, they met Queen Victoria who was fascinated with the idea of arranging the giant wedding. The Queen's dressmaker made Anna's gown and the couple were married in the Queen's chapel.

The newlyweds continued to tour Europe and in 1872, Anna Swan gave birth to an eighteen pound still-born baby girl. The child was given to the London Hospital for research on giantism and the saddened pair returned to the States. Traveling through Ohio, they

stopped in Seville to visit an old sideshow friend and decided that this quiet little town was a perfect place to settle down and hopefully raise a family of giants. They bought land east of town and built an Italianate home one-third larger than normal scale to accommodate their size. It had fourteen foot ceilings and over eight foot tall doors. A special ten-foot bed was made for them and the local ladies made a large quilt to welcome them. Fine furnishings and marble mantles imported from Europe made this one of Seville's finest homes.
In 1879, Anna had a second baby. Three area doctors attended the difficult birth and Anna delivered a twenty-four pound, thirty-one inch baby boy. In anticipation, the Bates had a very large crib made for their baby, but it was never used. The baby lived only eleven hours and Anna's dream for a family and Captain Bates' hopes for creating a new line of giants were dashed.

They continued to live in Seville but joined assorted circus groups when they needed money. As the years passed, Anna established a reputation as a pleasant but large Victorian lady who did good works for the church. Captain Bates became known for his violent temper which landed him in court more than once. But he did enjoy the Seville children, lifting them high over his head for a special thrill.

Anna died in 1899 at the age of fifty-one. Captain Bates, distraught with his loss, ordered a life-sized figure from Europe to mark her grave in Seville's Mound Hill Cemetery. Bates, "though still filling engagements as a circus attraction, took great pleasure in raising pedigreed livestock on his farm, Clydesdales and Norman horses, and shorthorn cattle". He later married the local Baptist minister's daughter, who was a little over five feet tall. Bates died in 1919 and was buried next to his made-to-order wife and their baby boy. Their custom-made home was razed in the 1950s, but the barn with his name and the date "1883" still stands.

William Bowen was born in York Township in 1853. While a student at Oberlin College, he sustained a football injury and had to have a foot amputated. He went to Hawaii as a missionary, accepted a job in a relative's sugar plantation, and prospered. He eventually owned the plantation, and while he did not actually know how many acres he owned, he employed over 2700 workers. He owned the railroad and steamship lines that shipped his products. The "Sugar King" died as one of the world's wealthiest men, but his sons became missionaries rather than follow him into business.

John A. Clark was born on a Guilford Township farm in 1837. He was educated at the Seville Academy and became a well-known public servant in Wadsworth, serving as mayor as well as superintendent of schools. He was editor of the Wadsworth *Enterprise* which ran its first issue in 1866. His *Young Folks' Gem* had 250,000 subscribers by 1875, representing every state "and territory" in the Union, and Canada–the largest juvenile paper in the world.

M.D. Tyler was a Seville beekeeper and "philosopher". He knew just how many trips a bee must make to gather an ounce of honey, and how the Queen and "all her little Amazon bees" conducted themselves. Five-foot-tall Henry Beech was an uneducated veterinarian who treated animals by letting them wander around the fields until they came to the plant that could cure them. Hinckley native Rowena Sweet was a noted temperance speaker and was the first woman in the country to be elected mayor. In one remarkable family, Lu Washburn was an expert botanist and experimental gardener for the A.I. Root Company. Her sister Sarah was an ornithologist who specialized in the birds of Northeastern Ohio. Their father Alva Washburn was a mechanic who invented a polishing machine for the Hollow Ware Foundry, a newspaper folding machine, and a comb foundation roller for his friend, A.I. Root. He was confined to his bed for the last several years of his life but repaired clocks and watches while lying on his back.

Vernacular Architecture

Vernacular houses are local variations of the high style designs built by urban and wealthy homeowners. These homes may be small or even humble, but still satisfy the hallmarks of good architecture: beauty, convenience, and durability. While upper-class and architect-designed homes were likely to follow pure style, regional craftsmen influenced by local traditions tended to translate fully developed styles into local folk art forms. Leaving the text-book characteristics to the architects and trained designers, they built homes of much charm and commodity. Many of the county's most attractive houses derive their beauty from the naiveté of their design.

Vernacular architecture is so ordinary in its own environment that it is often unappreciated. Materials or style traits which seem to be particular to a small area in Medina County include red slate roofs in York and Liverpool townships, square silos through the mid-section of the county, and brick houses in the vicinity of Valley City. Several Greek Revival houses in Medina, York, and Hinckley Townships have "Blakeslee" doors, a particular variety of trabeated-arch door named for the presumed nineteenth-century architect, Burritt Blakeslee.

In Wadsworth Township, brick houses and school buildings are plentiful. This may be attributed to a substantial German population familiar with masonry construction or a well-to-do-citizenry. The primary cause, however, was the abundance of coal in the region. Coal brought the railroad, and in turn, they both brought many businesses demanding bricks for their manufacturing plants. Several brick companies went up, the first in 1875, making bricks readily available.

In the decade between 1870 and 1880, hundreds of commercial buildings and houses were built in the county, particularly around Medina Square which had to be rebuilt after the devastating fire of 1870. While both the Second Empire and the Italianate styles were popular during that decade throughout the United States, the Italianate was much more popular in Medina County. For some reason, the Italianate style caught the fancy and met the needs of the county's citizens, and many were built as opposed to very few mansard-roofed ones.

A house in Mallet Creek, York Township.

The availability of materials. local building techniques, the individuality of design of a particular architect or carpenter, and regional design tastes all can effect architectural styles.

The shotgun house is named for the way the rooms line up in a row. The plan, allowing sunlight and air into each room, developed in the temperate climate of the Amer-ican South. Such houses are rare in Medina County, but this little story-and-a-loft example with its turned porch posts and balusters is a charming example. It is located in Brunswick Township.

A modest farmhouse becomes a little Greek Revival temple with the addition of a heavy entablature, Doric pilasters, a shallow gable roof, and classical proportions.

Medina County still has a large Amish community in its southwestern townships. The Amish house follows building traditions used a century ago. The shallow gable roofline and six-over-six windows survive from the Greek Revival period, but without any of the decorative elements. The saltbox lean-to addition adds easily heated, convenient space. Early chimneys were usually built within the wall to conserve heat and dissipate it throughout the house, but by this time chimneys are used only as flues for stoves.

James Whiteside, an early Guilford Township settler, arrived in 1819. He drove the Seville-to-Cleveland stage coach in the 1820s. He was also the carpenter of this Greek Revival house. It was built about 1830, and was known as the Crawford Homestead for many years. Since the turn of the century, it has been moved twice to avoid encroaching traffic. The triangular swell over the windows echoes a Greek pediment. The charming doorway owes more to the whimsy of the builder than to the decorative vocabulary of the Greek Revival style.

This cross-gable house was built in Lodi in 1888 at a taxable value of $350. At this time, the average non-agricultural wage was less than $400 per year. A hint of gingerbread decorates the vergeboard and the lintels of this rather plain house. There is a blind or false window to maintain the symmetry of the exterior, although the other shutters have been lost. Standing-seam roofs were available in Medina after about 1886 and were valued for their longevity and fire prevention capabilities. The angled corners of the gable peaks add interest to the symmetry of the house and roofline.

D.A. Parmalee owned the grist mill in Liverpool Center (now Valley City). In 1884 he built this two-and-a-half story Victorian house with sawtooth porch and window trim, cross gable plan, and a decorative wrought iron fence. The little shed-roofed porch shields separate entrances into the family and Sunday parlors.

William Strosaker built this Liverpool Township house in the 1880s. His son, Dr. Charles Strosacker, founder of the Dow Chemical Company, was born here. Stylistically, it is a mixture of types: it has an Italianate square porch, rounded windows, and bay window, and a lancet window and peaked roof on the addition from the Gothic Revival style. Screen doors were available in Medina after 1880.

The Farmhouse

During the last half of the nineteenth century, most Medina County citizens lived on farms. Some were poor families trying to eke out a living on the land they had recently settled. Contemporary accounts relate that many farmers had a poor standard of living, continuing to make their own cloth and cowhide boots, and eating a diet of salted codfish and whatever they could grow. Rude cabins sheltered these families throughout the Victorian era, although communities liked to boast that the log cabins in their neighborhood were long gone.

Many Medina farmers, however, were relatively well off after the Civil War. The average farm was just under fifty acres, and the railroad gave them a market for all the crops and livestock they could raise. Any farm over twenty acres needed additional workers, and in 1870 one-third of all Americans earned their living on the farm. By 1885, the average Medina County farm was eighty-five acres.

Farmhouses differed greatly from urban ones. They were generally much larger owing in part to the extra bedrooms for hired hands and larger families. The farm kitchen was also larger than its urban counterpart; it served as the main room of the house and was an efficient activity center with its own exterior door. Farm ideals were not city ideals. While city houses were not meant to be self-sufficient, the farm was a processing center for water, milk, smoked meats, cold storage, firewood, soap, jam, butter, honey, maple syrup, fruits, vegetables and herbs. Summer kitchens, washhouses, butchering sheds, smokehouses, sugarhouses and other outbuildings were built in the farmyard to keep heat, smoke, and the danger of fire away from the house.

Some farmers built their houses in the center of their property, far from the road but centrally located to woodlot, water supply, fields, and barns. This is common in Wadsworth Township. Most farmers built their houses directly on the main road to display them to the rest of the community. Farm families were justifiably proud of their complex of buildings. There must have been some truth to the adage that you could tell who "ruled the roost", the farmer or his wife, depending on whether the farmhouse or the outbuildings were in

better condition. There are still many barns in the county that have the name of the owner and date of construction spelled out in the roof slates. A.E. "Ed" Ritter learned the trade of laying metal and slate roofs as a young man in Spencer. After his marriage, he relocated to Medina and formed a partnership in Berry and Ritter Hardware. He laid virtually every slate roof in the county, and his daughter Letha Ritter Waltz remembers him laying out the patterns on the dining room table. In spite of his having only a fifth-grade education, he was able to figure the materials so closely that there was very little waste. Ritter also gilded the steeple of St. Martin's Church, hiding the sheets of gold in the pedestal base of his oak dining table at night.

Farmers were quite progressive, embracing new, efficient methods and equipment for house and barn. The ever-increasing mechanization of the farm—there were 10,00 reapers in Ohio by 1857—meant houses with fewer bedrooms to house farmhands after the turn of the century. The home manufacture of some products (soap, butter) stopped as cheap, mass-produced goods and products became readily available.

The farmer quite often was both designer and builder of his own house. Farm journals such as *Ohio Farmer* and *The Rural New Yorker* offered plans for houses and ideas for modernization. Every issue printed layouts and drawings sent by farmers who had built or designed or daydreamed about their own homes. There was a keen interest in comfort, convenience, and culture. A large parlor, signifying the civility of the farm family and offering a quiet, formal room away from the activity centers of the house, was part of the floor plan of rural houses until the turn of the century.

The Stick Style house is often considered to be a cross between the Gothic Revival and Queen Anne styles. The steep gable roof, decorative vergeboard cutwork trim and pendant on this house are reminiscent of Gothic style characteristics. The siding is laid in a herringbone pattern under the windows. This Montville Township farmhouse was built in the 1880s by E.R. Culver who had a large sugar bush on his 109-acre farm.

This fine brick farmhouse, like many in Wadsworth Township, was built a great distance from the road but convenient to the barn, wood supply, outbuildings, and water supply. The current owner of this farmhouse believes that it was built from bricks fired on the site. Some bricks are stamped with the date "1878".

The two-and-a-half story cross-gable Victorian house has hewn stone keystones and lintels and gingerbread trim. The porch posts are champfered, or angled, to add decorative interest. Narrow beaded panelling was often used for ceilings and kitchen, hallway, and porch walls in the nineteenth century.

The farm, once the most common source of livelihood in the county, is quickly being replaced by the "Planned Comm-unity". Modern and well painted buildings and outbuildings which denoted the "tidiness, thrift and prosperity of the owner" were once common in Medina County; certainly a fitting description of this farm complex built by Daniel Rohn.

Rohn arrived in Wadsworth Township with his family in the 1850s. The Rohns were part of the westward migration of Pennsylvania immigrants who settled in the southeast corner of Medina County. When Daniel married in 1861, he bought several small parcels of land and created this farmstead. He and his wife lived in a log house until 1874 when they built this two-story home in the traditional Greek Revival style.

Daniel's only son died at an early age, so upon Daniel's death, his eldest daughter and her husband left their sod house in Nebraska to take over the family homestead. The farm is still operated by Rohn's descendants.

The Rohn house has simple Greek Revival detailing but two-over-two windows which belie its late construction date. The foundation stones were quarried from the north pasture on the property. The picket fence, with cherry posts and spindles that were turned on a foot-powered lathe, is over a century old.

In 1889, itinerant artist F.A. Brader executed a 34 by 50 inch pencil drawing of the farm complex. The buildings remain intact and in use today. An 1879 barn, a wagon shed, a small outbuilding used for washing and butchering and a brick smoke house still stand. The tobacco barn stored the leaf tobacco grown here and marketed for cigar wrappers. The "necessary" or privy was a Works Projects Administration Depression-era project and is fondly called "Roosevelt's Monument".

The Rohn farm had is own orchard, vineyard, and extensive fruit and vegetable gardens. Family ledgers indicate that few trips were made into Wadsworth Village for store-bought supplies. As depicted in the Brader drawing, the Rohn farmstead was a model of industry and efficiency.

Barns

When the settlers arrived, their first task was to provide shelter for themselves. Any livestock they owned wandered through the dense forest with large bells to indicate their location, but the early farmers soon learned that their animals needed more permanent shelter. Bears and wolves attacked their stock and there were occasions when small children were lost in the woods while looking for an errant cow. It was common for a farmer to build a timber frame barn before a permanent house for his family, since the family's welfare was so dependent upon the good health and safety of the animals.

The first barns may have been just small lean-to sheds protected by a stump and brush stockade, soon replaced by log barns. N.B. Northrop raised the first barn in Medina Village in 1817; the first Wadsworth barn went up in 1819. Unlike the log cabin, the log barn was unchinked for ventilation. Until the 1880s, the predominant style was a simple log or frame shed where the animals shared space with grain and implements.

Once the land was settled and the homestead secure, large, new barns were the mark of the farm's prosperity. By the end of the Civil War, the farmer was "king and barns were the palaces of America". In Medina County over five hundred barns were raised in the last two decades of the nineteenth century. In the 1880s the new "Sweitzer Barn" or bank barn became popular throughout the county. The design of a bank barn separated the animals from the work areas and opened up new space for activities. Introduced by Germans from Pennsylvania, this compact, efficient style provided an upper floor for threshing and grain storage and a lower level of stalls for the animals. Many existing barns were converted into bank barns by raising them on a stone foundation and grading a ramp to the upper level. Bank barns were well built of the finest materials and cost about $3000 to build in the late nineteenth century. An Ohio bank barn which burned cost over $900,000 to reproduce in 1994.

When he planned a new barn, the farmer cut and hewed the support beams and let them cure for a year. Then he built a fieldstone or ashlar foundation, laid down the wood flooring, and assembled the beams into *bents*. A bent was the support structure of one side of the barn. Now all was ready for the raising. People would gather to work and to socialize. News stories tell of as many as two hundred on hand: the men worked on the barn and the women cooked. One by one the bents were raised by long poles and brute strength and secured to the barn floor. At the end of the day, one brave soul took the ritual walk across the roof's ridge pole to declare the barn raised. The finish work of siding, doors, and roofing was completed later by the host farmer or a professional builder. David Richert was the expert barn contractor in Medina County until he was killed by a falling beam in Weymouth in 1891.

Accidents were common at barn raisings in part because of the flow of alcohol. The hosts supplied the drink and their friends and neighbors provided the muscle. In the southern part of the county, there was little socializing between the "Yankee" and the Pennsylvania Dutch, but when a Dutchman raised a barn, all attended because of the promise of good beer. The first recorded barn dance in Medina county was in 1889. After that date, new barns were commonly celebrated with large dances, a practice begun in Medieval times to tamp and pack the barn's earthen floor in preparation for threshing.

Other agricultural buildings were necessary to the farm, including sheep sheds, corncribs, springhouses, and other outbuildings. In 1881, S.J. Shane of Chatham built the county's first windmill, and others quickly followed. The windmills powered machinery to cut grain and chop fodder and wood. The first silo was built in York in 1889. Prior to that time, farmers stored feed in an underground pit covered with tree roots or branches. A pioneer recalled losing five acres of wheat to squirrels because he had no suitable storage area. Until the appearance of the silo, farmers could not securely store milk-producing feed through the winter and many cows went dry until spring.

From the early settlements to the present, agriculture has supported Medina County. A farmer's worth and success were measured by the appearance of modern, well-kept buildings and equipment. Healthy farms meant a healthy economy and that Medina was a growing and prospering county.

A proud farmer trimmed his 1850s barn with a heavy entablature and returns to match his Greek Revival house in Westfield Township. The barn still has vestiges of its original red paint.

This small barn would have housed the horse, tack, and feed for the homeowner's carriage. The jutting roof finial facilitated loading hay into the loft.

This Spencer Township barn has louvered windows and arched doors. In the late nineteenth century it was used as a cheese factory for the Warner and Webster Company. The dairy industry was for many years one of the mainstays of the county's economy. The first cheese was made in the county in 1815, and by 1873 Chatham Township alone annually produced $400,000 worth of milk and milk products from 1200 to 1500 cows.

Small outbuildings served a variety of purposes on the farm. Storage sheds, springhouses, washhouses, smokehouses, corn cribs, outhouses, and summer kitchens allowed the farm family to be efficient and self-sustaining. This Westfield Township outbuilding has board-and-batten siding, known for its weather repelling capabilities.

Henry Snyder's bank barn in Spencer Township has a protective overhang on the south side which shelters the livestock from winter winds. Built in 1889, this barn features both cupolas and dormers which provide ventilation. It was thought that ample ventilation deterred lightning, but for added protection, lightning rods were often used.

Large farms had a complex of buildings to house animals, tools, and feed. The finest materials—chestnut siding and slate roof tiles—and regular painting and maintenance mean that many barns are still in use and in excellent condition throughout Medina County.

Barn roofs proudly proclaiming the date of construction and the name of the owner were common throughout the county just a short time ago. High maintenance costs, the abandonment of farms to urban encroachment, and the replacement of draft animals with machine power have threatened the American barn.

Schweitzer or bank barns facilitated the loading of hay into the loft, then utilized gravity to lower it to the livestock on the first floor. Bank barns were very popular with farmers, and many existing barns were transformed into bank barns after 1890.

The E. Fahrion barn in York Township has an early, square silo. It is thought that round silos prevented the spontaneous combustion of grain trapped in the corners. Square silos are angled off inside as a result. Barns with square silos are common in York, Medina, and Litchfield townships in the northern and middle parts of the county.

Charles Camp of Homer Township bred first class blooded road horses, percheron draft horses, and trotters. He shipped his thoroughbred horses throughout the country and advertised through catalogues and newspapers. This cattle barn, built in 1888, has decorative windows, ventilators, and trim. The disengaged silo was a later addition. The Camp farmstead has been lovingly maintained by subsequent owners and is one of the most beautiful in the county.

Barns continued to be built by hewn log construction into the twentieth century. People gathered from near and far to help. One hundred and fifty neighbors helped William Hood raise his barn in Bagdad in 1890. This bank barn, shown under construction and soon after completion, is owned by the Vargo family and still stands in Hinckley Township.

There is a saying that round barns "kept the devil from hiding in the corners". In practical terms, they were well-lit and well-ventilated. This Harrisville Township barn with a little octagonal cupola was used as a chicken house and was built about 1895.

The Bostwick Brothers of Westfield Township built three tobacco barns in 1892. Their farm, situated in the southern part of the county on low-lying land, was well-suited for growing tobacco. The cigar industry flourished in Guilford, Westfield, and Liverpool townships from the 1880s until after World War I when the cigarette replaced the cigar in popularity. The 1000 foot long barn is well ventilated for drying and curing tobacco. This is the only remaining original barn; two others were lost in fires in 1893.

Tobacco farmers bringing in a Medina County crop at the turn of the century.

Roads and Bridges

Smooth, hard-surfaced roads and convenient bridges are taken for granted today. It is difficult to imagine a time when roads were often impassable due to swollen rivers and flooded farm fields. Recreational travel and even the shipment of goods was curtailed for weeks on end. In 1830, Neal and Company opened a stage line between Wayne, Medina and Cuyahoga Counties but in bad weather, it could take fourteen hours for the trip from Cleveland to Medina. Heavy loads, like building materials, were hauled and delivered to a site over frozen winter roads; it would be impossible once spring thaws came. Roads and bridges were actually more passable in winter when ice and snow were packed rather than removed. Sleighs were used for travel and sleds moved goods and materials. Huge logs drawn along by horse and sleigh tamped and leveled the snow. Winters with little snowfall could be problematical. A history of Ohio written in 1833 laments the fact that recent winters had been mild and there was so much more good snow for sledding in "the old days". Spring rains and thawing snow made driving a miserable chore, with water-filled ruts and pot holes trapping wooden wheels. In summer months, heat and sun brought choking dust. Mrs. R.P. Loveland died of "nervous prostration" due to a long drive over bad roads after a visit to her sister in Wayne County in the 1870s.

Heavy loads made hill climbing so difficult that roads were often built around them. A farmer or tradesman could not hope to make a profit if it took him too long to get his goods to market. Reimer Road near Beach Road in Wadsworth Township and Route 303 just west of Hinckley were cut around steep hills until dynamite was available at the end of the nineteenth century.

Wooden plank and macadam roads were not known in the county's early days. Brush was cleared and land was leveled with huge logs drawn along by draft animals. Until the 1860s, roads were built by pulling a plow and scraper along the roadside, clearing a deep ditch for water run-off and throwing the dirt onto the roadbed. In principle, this carriageway high above the water-filled ditches provided additional protection from the mud, but in theory, the soft earth soon water-logged and in wet weather "stopped them in their tracks". Boardwalks, later replaced by flagstone and then concrete, were built for pedestrians.

In the settlement years, local citizens joined forces to assist in the building of a bridge. All males "aged twenty-one years having resided in the county three months" were required to contribute two days to road building, commutable by paying seventy-five cents per day. Many days would be wholly devoted to construction of a bridge that would likely be "carried away by a succeeding freshet". Flooding was frequent before culverts were built and tiles were laid to divert water. Repair, improvement, and maintenance were ongoing tasks. Later, workers were hired to build and maintain bridges, although they were paid in part with food in those cash-poor times. At the end of the nineteenth century, Paul C. Parker and Charles Reutter were two well-known bridge builders in the county, working in both stone and wood. Bridges with the date and Reutter's signature can still be found in Harrisville and Medina townships.

This covered bridge over the Rocky River near Weymouth survived a major flood in 1913 and was the last one standing in the county. Covered bridges were expected to last about 20 years, but one built on this site by P.C. Parker in 1872 fell within three months and had to be replaced. It was built of white oak, valued for its strength and resilience, and was 75 feet long, 14 feet wide, and 12 feet high.

Stone viaducts and bridges were known in the United States after 1829. Bridges were generally made of cast concrete after 1900, however, because stone and the wood used for framing became too expensive. Natural stone is extremely durable, however, and has a beauty not attainable with concrete. This 150 foot long bridge over the Black River in Harrisville Township was built in 1890-92. It was a source of curiosity and pride for the community. The *Gazette* reported that on one day eight hundred people walked to the viaduct to view the progress. Nineteen-year-old Morris Northrop hauled water to the workers and died when he fell seventy-five feet from the top of the bridge. It is listed on the National Register of Historic Places and is still in use.

After the 1850s, railroad loads were too heavy for timber-framed bridges. The iron bridge was invented in England for use on railroad lines. Iron is many times stronger than wood, and its resiliency and resistance to shearing make it valuable for trestle construction. This bridge built by the Canton Bridge Company in 1893 still stands over the Rocky River in Montville Township.

Commercial Buildings

Many settlers bought frontier land on credit and had to work for others to support their families before they could raise crops of their own to sell or trade. Goods and services were procured through the barter system, but commerce began in the earliest days of settlement as the pioneers took advantage of any opportunity that would bring a few coins to their pockets. After all, the settlers came west to progress and to prosper. Justus Warner of Liverpool Township is a good example. He paid local Native Americans to show him the salt springs near his "cut". He then traveled to Canton, purchased fifty iron kettles and began boiling down the salt water. In this way, he enabled the pioneers to preserve meat through the winter and opened this area's first business.

Others soon followed with their own means of making money and breaking the barter cycle. In 1820, the principal Ohio products were flour, whiskey, salt, and maple sugar. By mid-century, Ohio was the center of the dairy and Merino wool industries. There were 97,656 sheep in Medina County alone by 1861. In 1828, Hinckley had a three-story woolen mill forty feet square, the largest commercial building in the county. Asheries were another industry scattered throughout the forest. As the forests were cleared and burned, the trees were hauled to local asheries where they were further processed into "black and white salts" and pearl ash. These products were then carried to Cleveland by ox teams and then east to the iron industries.

In 1823, Robert Usher Richards and his brother Steward built a large factory for making pails, ferkins, half-bushels, pecks, and wooden bottles on a steam-powered lathe. Their business was ruined when they failed to find a way to dry the products evenly, causing leaky splits and cracks. At the same time, William Harrison Seymour went East to study chemistry in an unsuccessful attempt to make sugar from potatoes.

As the trees gave way to the ax, mills sprang up on Medina County's streams and rivers. One of the first was the Seymour and Doane sawmill in Weymouth in 1817. Sawmills, gristmills and carding mills offered the basic needs of building materials, flour and cloth to the scattered citizens. Before the mills, settlers had to travel for hours to Middlebury (now Akron) to grind their grain just to sustain their families. So millers were an essential part of the early commercial scene. Though few mills remain, there are still remnants of the mill races and foundation stones which serve as a reminder of this early industry.

Peddlers sold tinware and notions door-to-door. The earliest store in the county opened in Brunswick in 1819, and general merchandise stores were common throughout the county by the 1830s. Stores and other support businesses – tanneries, cobblers, blacksmiths, small foundries, cabinet makers, coopers, chandlers, wheel-wrights– made a variety of goods and services available and were standard enterprises in any 19th century community.

At one time, Liverpool Township was the center of a variety of commerce and industry. Warner's salt works, Pritchard's foundry, Parmalee's carding mill and cloth dressing factory that put out 10,000 yards of cloth a year, Carr's planing mill making washing machines and bedsprings, and Luther Welton's Windsor chair factory were among the many businesses. Liverpool also seemed to have a corner on the grain alcohol enterprise. According to the 1881 *History of Medina County*, there were at least three distillers that bought corn and rye from the local farmers and converted it into liquor that "was drank as fast as it was made". In the 1830s, John Groll added strychnine to his brew for flavor and a "staggering sensation". Alcohol consumption in the

early nineteenth century was frightfully high, about four times that of today, and was responsible for crime, violence, and accidents. In the 1870s, Medina's "Temperance Ladies" marched through the streets condemning strong drink. But until that time, it was an accepted business that gave the farmers an additional market for their crops.

Until the 1870s these commercial ventures primarily filled the needs of the local citizens. Aside from the canal locks in Summit County, there was no way to market goods elsewhere. A large number of consumers had to be reached to bring prosperity to the producers. The coming of the railroads in the 1860s gave the county an expanded market for their goods and resources. In Wadsworth Township, coal deposits heated only local homes until the railroad created vast markets and brought about small coal mining villages, special railroad spurs and resultant industries such as Ohio Match and Ohio Salt.

When the railroad came to Medina in 1871, it gave J.R. Holcomb the opportunity to expand his small printing operation in York Township. By 1875, he was shipping his *Teacher's Guide* and other educational aides throughout the country. Eventually, he moved his expanding company to Cleveland where it remains today. A.I. Root saw the same opportunity for growth when he shifted from the jewelry business on the square to manufacturing bee supplies and catalog marketing.

Behind this drive for growth and development was the local press. The first paper in Medina was the Ohio *Free Press,* established in 1832, which eventually became the Medina County *Gazette*. The early papers were essentially voices for political parties, but they did provide advertising space and often promoted the county's enterprising citizens. In some cases, the editor expanded his business to include other projects. At one time Medina County had three national publications printed within its boundaries: John Clark's *Young Folks Gems* for children in Wadsworth which had a national circulation of 400,000, J.R. Holcomb's guide and A.I. Root's *Gleanings in Bee Culture.*

Before the Civil War, Medina County architecture was primarily log or the classic designs of the Federal and Greek Revival styles. During the War, new building nearly came to a halt. Labor was scarce, as the county sent over 550 men to the War. Of that number, 154 did not return and another 151 were wounded or disabled by injuries or chronic illness. There were also economic disruptions when the lucrative war contracts dried up and crop prices plummeted. The difficult times continued through 1873 when a severe depression struck the country. Added to this turmoil was the devastation suffered during Medina's 1870 fire. The town center was virtually destroyed just when everyone was trying to recuperate from the economic effects of the

The village of Seville in 1857.

War. On the positive side, new railroads now enabled Medina County products and goods to go beyond the local area and opened new markets to products, crops, and resources. A sense of pride and determination took over as the community rebuilt its burnt center. A.I. Root caught the fever and moved his new bee industry to the west side of town, providing room for future growth. John Smart settled here from New York, helped to develop the Hollow Ware Foundry and built a beautiful home which still stands on North Elmwood Street.

In 1898, the *Gazette* printed a special edition called "Thriving Medina and its Prospects". It was a promotional piece extolling Medina's clean water, reasonable freight rates and low energy costs from local coal deposits. It also mentioned the secure banking institutions, including Old Phoenix bank. To today's reader, the most valuable aspect of the edition is the door-to-door description of Medina's commercial blocks with the business and building histories. It is an excellent picture of late nineteenth-century Medina, rebuilt after the 1870 fire and ready for progress and prosperity. The United States became a viable entity in the world's marketplace and new styles in dress, architecture, and furnishings were readily embraced. By the mid-1870s, Medina began its building boom with the Italianate style. The prosperous 1880s brought elaborate Queen Anne, Stick, Shingle, and Eastlake style homes. There was no longer a time gap between metropolitan and rural styles. Medina County left the pioneer age as it moved into a new era.

Richard Lampson owned much of York Township and was one of the few landowners to actually reside here. He built his house and tavern in Mallet Creek in about 1836 and died here at the age of 90 in 1866. The simple vernacular Federal style building was razed in 1987.

Milo and Horace Gibb built the first "public house" (inn and tavern) in Sharon Center in 1836. After it outgrew its usefulness as an inn, it was made into a house and stood as a Sharon landmark until it was razed in the 1990s.

"Billy" Bloomfield's sawmill at Weymouth, Ohio about 1860

Weymouth, one of the earliest and largest Medina County villages in the settlement years, had two industries. Seymour and Doane built one of the earliest sawmills there, operated by a succession of owners until the end of the nineteenth century.

A second enterprise, the Weymouth stone quarry, produced a fine-grained, drab-colored stone, more suitable for cemetery monuments than for construction. The quarry opened in the 1840s and it was thought that the two foot thick vein was an endless supply that would last "forever", but it closed after the turn of the century.

"Downtown" Spencer at the turn of the century.

Lodi's three-story brick block was built for J. W. Wolcott in 1866. It has cast iron columns which were not available until about 1860. Soon, iron and then steel would be used to frame buildings and could support higher and higher skyscrapers in cities whose population and commerce warranted them. This building was later known as the Ainsworth Block and was part of the estate endowed to Ainsworth Lodge, a home for elderly women familiarly known as the Old Ladies' Home.

The little village of Weymouth supported two general stores at one time. Tiernan's store, above, had a dance hall on the second floor. It closed in the 1940s, and was razed. The extension that served as a home for the shopkeeper was moved back a few feet and has been converted into a house.

The Crooks/Einhart store had the Weymouth post office. It was closed in 1991.

In the early years after America won its independence from Britain, every town had an "American House" inn. Medina's first American House was a frame one in the Federal style built in 1830 on the north side of the square. It was later replaced with a three-story brick building that had thirty sleeping rooms. During the 1870 fire, blankets and quilts were laid on the roof and kept wet with salt and water. The building was saved, but the furnishings were badly damaged when they were hurredly moved from the building. In 1872, owner Phil Warner ran the "Medina omnibus down to the cars" at the depot. The porch and second story verandah were added in 1875 and were a favorite gathering spot for Medina's "sidewalk superintendents" until the hotel was razed in 1954.

Liverpool Center, later known as Valley City, at one time had five cigar factories. Charles Hoppe, from Saxony, Germany, operated a cigar manufacturing plant in this false front shop. His leading brand was "Golden Seal of Cuba".

The Phoenix Block draped in mourning for the funeral of founder H.G. Blake. In this photograph taken in 1876, six years after the great fire, the Phoenix building stands alone on the south side of the square.

Harrison G. Blake founded the Old Phoenix Bank in 1857. At that time, the bank consisted of an iron safe in Blake's law office in the first Phoenix Block, an 1850s Federal style building which was located on the site of the present Phoenix building. From there, he accepted deposits, discounted "good paper", and bought and sold gold. The "good paper" were bank notes without National bank support but backed by some strong, stable bank. At that time, currency varied by community and its value changed weekly.

After the 1870 fire, a second Phoenix block "rose from the ashes" and the Phoenix bank opened in the east half of the first floor. In 1873, in response to a severe economic depression, the bank joined the National Banking System and became the Phoenix National Bank. A new charter changed the name to Old Phoenix National Bank in 1893. By the twentieth century, Old Phoenix had survived the Civil War, a major fire, and two serious economic depressions. Today, it remains an important part of Medina's banking and commerce scene almost 140 years after its founding.

Many merchants lived in apartments above their stores, or rented out the space for additional income. This mercantile building in Seville, McDowell's Grocery, has four oriel windows (cantilevered bay windows) letting more light and a little extra space into the apartment's rooms. The brickwork has been laid in a decorative garland pattern, adding interest to the plain wall surface. Plate glass windows, which cost about $25 each, were seen as a marketing tool attracting customers to the store's wares. Advertising signage indicates the wide variety of goods available as a general store.

Ramson Riley and his son Wallace had a general store in Hinckley Center. It was directly adjacent to Bronger's store, but differed in that it sold meat and served as the post office, while Bronger's general merchandise store sold medicines and drugs. The Maccabees, a fraternal organization, held society meetings over the store. This transitional building still has the shallow gable roof, 6/6 lights, and symmetry of the Greek Revival style, but is Victorianized with Gothic gingerbread, a finial ornament, turned columns, drip molding, and a variety of colors.

VIEW ON CELERY FARM.

The "Muck Angels" worked the gardens that were reclaimed out of the Harrisville Township swamps. The first one opened in 1887 with 573 acres. By 1911, Horr Warner Company (later known as the Garden Isle farm) had four farms totaling over 1200 acres and hired up to one thousand seasonal workers. They were the largest growers of onions in the United States and exported vegetables throughout the country and abroad. They also grew potatoes, cabbage, and enough celery "to make nerve tonic for the world". The "million dollar kettle bowl" supported other businesses such as coopers and crate makers. The Alderfer Crate Company in Sharon supplied them with as many as 1500 packing crates a day. A new post office, Haldo, opened in 1893 to serve the vast gardens.

American architect Henry Hobson Richardson (1838-1886) invented the style known as Richardsonian Romanesque. Horizontal stone bands and massive stone arches are used to create an authoritative, masculine style commonly used for commercial and public architecture during the 1890s. The Medina County *Gazette* building was designed and built by the Gruninger Brothers in 1894-95 in time for the 60th anniversary of the paper. The three-story brick block has a stone front and lintels, dentil molding decorating the cornice, an oriel window, and a Romanesque-arched arcade. It had a gas-fired press, a gas lighting machine, and was heated by steam. On the second floor, George F. High operated a jewelry business and Miss Della Hartman had a music studio.

Charles Hazel and Herbert Bennet opened this general store in Valley City about 1890. The house, of older vintage, was moved to the site and added to the rear of the shop later.

The false front style was used in Western towns to make simple frontier shops look more important and urbanized. The idea spread to the rest of the country after the Gold Rush.

In 1820, Samuel and James Fowler purchased 17,000 acres of land in the Western Reserve sight unseen from the Connecticut Land Company. They owned most of Westfield Township and 4600 acres in Lafayette Township (taxed at $34.45 per annum). When they came to Medina in 1826 and saw their land, they demanded another seven hundred acres in compensation for the large lake which covered so much of their property. Before long, this 385 acre lake became popular as a resort for cottagers and excursion parties and was also used as a source of ice and fish. The interurban electric train made several trips to and from Cleveland each day. Chippewa Lake was one of the earliest resorts in the country, opening in 1870, and did not close until the 1970s.

The Stick Style dance hall at the park was replaced by a newer one in 1922.

N.W. Hower opened a general store in 1837. By 1896 his sons had stores in Lodi and Burbank selling dry goods, clothing, and shoes. This Italianate building in Lodi has a decorated frieze band, paired brackets supporting a wide overhang, and round-headed windows. Large plate glass windows allowed the shopkeepers to advertise their wares. the store is still operated by members of the Hower family.

An 1872 *Gazette* article complained that "the streets of Lodi are one vast cow yard" and called for legislation to forbid cattle in the town center.

This shop on South Court Street in Medina was rebuilt in the Italianate style after the fire of 1870. Decorative brackets and dentils support a heavy cornice, echoed in the galleried hood molding over the plate glass windows. Canvas awnings, often embellished with advertising signage, were in common use during summer months to cool the building's interior and protects the wares. This building housed Ida Cannon's grocery store for many years in the twentieth century.

Ephriam B. Brenner owned a saloon in Medina Village. At first, he refused to close his business in response to agitation by Women's Christian Temperance Union supporters, but was persuaded after they held repeated prayer and singing vigils on his steps. Driven out of business, he became a hotel keeper and landlord. His first hotel, the Eagle, was lost in the 1870 fire. The Gruninger Brothers replaced it with this Second Empire hotel on South Court Street in 1872. It has decorative brackets supporting a mansard-roofed cornice, engraved stone keystones, dormer windows with their own decorative roofs, metal grills on double doors, and patterned pentagonal roof slates.

Ohio Farmers' Insurance

The greatest enemy of the early farmer was fire. A spilled oil lamp or a lightening strike could destroy everything a family had. The newspapers were full of accounts of barns destroyed and families left without a home or means of support because there was no way to fight a fire. A few buckets of water from a cistern or well had little effect on a roaring blaze.

In the 1840s, an enterprising salesman came to Westfield Township to sell fire insurance. Subscribers soon discovered that their insurance premiums were phony pieces of paper from a bogus company. Local resident Jonathan Simmons traveled to New York to study the insurance business and encourage a company to locate in Medina County. After his trip, he concluded that it would be far easier to start a company at home than to depend upon outsiders. In 1847, a group of local farmers and businessmen met at Ben Austin's store on Westfield Circle and began the process of incorporating a new insurance business. By 1848, the Ohio Farmers' Insurance Company was chartered by the Ohio Legislature. State Representative H.G. Blake of Medina sponsored the bill.

In April, the original founders met and elected George Collier as the company's first president. By June there were enough insurance applications to warrant issuing the first policy. That went to Jonathan Simmons, the man who originally proposed founding a company. In those days prospective customers could buy their insurance literally "over the counter" at Austin's store. But as business increased, the office moved to a wing of the store and then to a small Greek Revival building. The company prospered primarily because there were no claims on the policies until after 1849. One sign of its success was the growing number of door plates attached to area homes to indicate that they were covered by Ohio Farmers' Insurance.

In 1856, the directors voted to build a "fireproof" brick office building. It was tiny but served for ten years with periodic additions that enlarged the original space. By this time, Amos G. Hawley was secretary of the company and lived upstairs in the new quarters. By 1880, even this structure was outgrown. A new building, completed in 1883, with its Medieval tower and mansard roof reflected the latest architectural designs and served as both company headquarters and community activity center for this company town.

But the most imposing building associated with Ohio Farmers' Insurance was the mansion built by Amos' son Amos Hoyt on the southwest side of the town circle. The Gruninger Brothers of Medina built it between 1886 and 1888. A.H. died two years later but his son Frank lived in the house until his death in 1946. Seven years later the company bought the property and razed it to make room for additional office space. In its day, the Hawley mansion was Medina County's most impressive home.

OFFICE OF OHIO FARMER INSURANCE CO LEROY, OHIO.

The *Gazette* thought that this "stately edifice towering toward the sky" was "Romanesque, not Moorish". Two pink marble pillars support the entrance canopy. The building had three Diebold safes and a gas Ruby furnace. George Lowe did the interior painting and varnishing, and Hobart and Blackford of Medina were responsible for the slate and tin work. The Ohio Farmers' Company building was completed in 1882. The ninety-foot Gothic tower, a mansard roof, and decorative iron fencing were removed in 1913.

The twenty-six room Queen Anne Hawley mansion had "artificial gas lighting, running water, beveled glass doors, interior bathrooms, and oak pocket doors". The Moorish onion dome, unique in Medina County, illustrates the Victorian penchant for adopting a variety of historical styles, however inappropriate. Hawley House, completed in 1888, was located on the southwest part of Westfield Circle, and was razed in 1953 for additional office space.

The A.I. Root Company

Amos Ives Root was one of Medina's finest eccentrics. Born in a log cabin in York Township in 1839, he was a frail child who used his wits to avoid tedious tasks and to earn spending money. He once rigged his mother's butter churn to a treadmill and at age sixteen devised a traveling show. He lectured on chemistry and electricity and captured the crowd with his magic "galvanized" slippers which jolted volunteers from the audience. He courted Susan Hall of Medina but her father thought that such a strange fellow was not a suitable match, so Root gave up his traveling show and learned the clock and jewelry business. His store was on the west side of the square on the site of Town Square Commons. At one time he employed twelve workers and melted down $500 worth of silver a week. And he won the hand of Susan Hall.

On a fateful day in 1865, A.I. Root became fascinated with a swarm of bees. He spent a full day traveling to Cleveland, finding a book on bees, and purchasing a queen bee for twenty dollars. In spite of everyone's misgivings, he had a barrel of honey and a bee colony by the end of the summer, and gave up the jewelry business to manufacture bee-keeping equipment. Bees were used for pollination as well as sweetener and a source of wax for jar and bottle seals, furniture polish, and lubricant. His company made extractor buckets, hives and smokers in the old jewelry shop. By 1870, Root had made his name. His articles in the *American Bee* were so well received that he founded his own journal in 1873. Five years later his expanding business needed new quarters. Root purchased the old fairgrounds on West Liberty Street and built his first "home for the honeybees", a ten by fourteen foot frame shed. Root produced 6000 pounds of honey from 48 colonies in the tiny space. To accommodate his growing business, Root put up a brick factory building in 1878. When the contractor demanded payment, Root did not have the funds. Earnest prayer brought a stranger who offered him five hundred dollars for his bee-keeping advice. In thanks, Root put a hive and "In God We Trust" on his building. In just eleven years, Root had six thousand colonies and was world renowned for his products and his expertise.

In 1882, A.I. and Susan Root built their grand brick Queen Anne home just west of the factory. As the family grew and prospered, their children became involved in the business and built homes on West Liberty, known to the town's people as "Rootville".

As the business grew, buildings were added to the complex. In 1890 a brick addition to the original plant had electric lights, indoor toilets, street lights, and a sprinkler system. Electricity was also extended to the Root houses and to the Medina Congregational Church.

Root, an early conservationist, planted basswood trees north of Medina to supply wood for his patented hives. He used the sawdust and shavings to fire the plant furnaces. Scrap wood was made into toys, a new line added to his growing catalogue of products. *Gleanings in Bee Culture* was printed

Gilt honeybees and skips adorn the lunette window of the sandstone 1890 A.I. Root building on West Liberty Street.

by windmill power.

His inventive nature never left him—he had the first bicycle in town, a French velocipede, which he practiced riding on the third floor of the Phoenix Block. In 1903, he had Medina's first automobile, an Oldsmobile. He was the first to write about the Wright brothers' flight. He became a friend of Wilbur and Orville Wright through his involvement with the Sunday School Movement and was invited to witness an early flight in Dayton. His account of the flight in *Gleanings in Bee Culture* went unnoticed until after the events at Kitty Hawk.

The unconventional Root may have been laughable if not for his success. An active, creative mind along with strong principles and hard work made him one of the county's leading citizens. Before his death in 1923 (sixty-one years after a doctor predicted it), A.I. wrote down his advice for success:

. Know everything there is to be known about the business you're in
. Avoid a rut as you would the pestilence
. Don't go into debt
. Don't be afraid to try new things
. Trust the Lord

W. Liberty Street, Medina, Ohio.

Rootville", on West Liberty Street just beyond the A.I. Root Company buildings, was illuminated by the dynamo at the Root plant. Arc lights lit the street with 2000 candle power. Root built the Colonial Revival house next to his own for his daughter Connie when she married A.L. Boyden in 1899. Sons Huber and Ernest and another daughter lived nearby.

Susan and A.I. Root built their Queen Anne house with Eastlake detailing in 1882-83. It cost $7080. The decorative brickwork is accentuated with sandstone lintels, sills, and keystones. The porch balusters were turned on a lathe. The sawtooth brickwork stringcourse is unusual but attractively breaks up the expanse of wall space. Segmented hood molding in varied shades of stone add decorative interest. The octagonal Queen Anne tower shelters a gazebo on the front porch. Tall, sculptural chimneys, iron cresting, and decorative bracketing at the edges of the roof lead the eye upward and accentuate the mass of the house.

John Brongers

John Brongers emigrated to America from Holland in 1863. While serving in the Civil War he befriended a fellow soldier, William Behr. In 1870, they settled in Hinckley, rented Charles Wood's general store on the northwest corner of the center, and opened for business. They sold dry goods, drugs, and groceries shipped from Cleveland by team. Behr soon sold out, but Brongers developed a lucrative business and became one of the village's leading citizens. In the early years, Brongers was a drinker. One day he cut a piece of yardage for a customer. Not realizing that he was tearing along the length, he damaged quite a few yards of goods. He stopped drinking that day and hung the cloth in his store as a reminder.

Brongers' store was in a Greek Revival building with a Victorian false front facade. It is still in use today as a 1990s variant of the "general store" selling FAXes, photo-copies, dog licenses, and lottery tickets as well as beverages, food and household items.

His family's first home was a small Greek Revival one, but Brongers was soon (1883) able to replace it with a commodious house in the latest style. The similarities between the Greek Revival and the Classical Revival are interesting to note. Both styles harken back to classical elements—pediment, entablatures, columns, the Greek orders—but the result is very different. Porch rails, large panes of plate glass, second story porches, and paired columns were not found before the Victorian Era. The most apparent difference—the bulky, irregular massing—was not possible before balloon frame construction. Returns built after the Civil War have an angled inside edge to divert water. By this time, soft woods were used in construction and they could not withstand the effects of standing water. Brongers had one of the first slate roofs in town– much more expensive than wood shingles but expected to last about thirty years. In fact, many slate roofs from the Victorian Era still serve today.

Brongers was well-liked in Hinckley and a generous benefactor to his community. He built a park on the southwest corner of town square as a pleasure ground and place for "Baptism in the brook". He had arrived in Hinckley with only "a pack on his back", and gratefully left his estate to the citizens of Hinckley Township when he died.

Mr. Brongers and his handsome family in their up-to-the-minute furnishings, attire, and poses.

Frank Leach

Frank Leach was born to O.N. and Electa Leach in Wellington in 1867. He came to Medina Village as a child and upon graduation from Medina High School, went to work in his father's clothing store as a tailor and salesman. The shop, on West Washington Street facing Medina Square (middle building below), sold clothing, men's furnishings, and "cloths". It was built by George Gruninger in 1879.

Frank was active in community affairs and business organizations, and also owned a bicycle shop with a "first class line of goods". In 1889, on the occasion of his marriage to Mary Sipher, Frank's father bought him a village lot for two hundred dollars and Frank built this English Cottage Stick Style house for his bride. It has decorative trusswork and bracketing and a large dormer adapted from the Shingle Style.

Frank and Mary had four children before Frank's untimely death of typhoid fever in 1902 at the age of thirty-five.

John and Barbara Renz

John and Barbara Renz were both born in Liverpool Township in 1838. Renz came to Medina in 1852, apprenticing in the harness trade with John Rettig. He worked for Rettig until 1867, when he entered into partnership with Ephriam Brenner. In 1893 he bought out Brenner's share and took two of his sons, Frank and Frederick, as partners. They carried not only harnesses but saddles, trunks, and other leather goods at their South Court Street store built in 1873. Renz considered himself to be "one of the finest mechanics" in Medina and displayed his finest work in showcases that are still in use in the building today. The Renz family continued to operate the store until the 1930s when the automobile and the Depression forced them out of business.

This house was built by Mr. and Mrs. Renz in celebration of their fiftieth wedding anniversary in 1910. It is transitional between the Queen Anne, with its large corner tower and stained glass windows, and Classical Revival with details which include an accentuated pediment, heavy cornice and entablature around the tower, Ionic capitals, Doric pilasters, and dentil molding.

Mr. and Mrs. Renz in 1860 and in 1910.

Classical Revival

During the last decades of the nineteenth century, the rambling Victorian styles held the American imagination. Rather than a single style, the Victorian was a profusion and confusion of styles. At the end of the century, however, popular taste reverted to a renewed appreciation of order and simplicity. A primary example is the Classical Revival style which retains some of the elements of the Queen Anne, notably large windows, porches, steep roofs, and towers, but utilizes new design elements and a simplified overall appearance. The Queen Anne period used some Classical features, but many more were added until a profusion of Greco-Roman decorative elements caused the new style to be named Classical Revival. Columns with Greek order capitals, pediments, entablatures, and pilasters are typical on this style of architecture. Large, open porches now showcase the front entry rather than serve as an outdoor extension to the living area. Porch railings and balusters comprised of turned stiles were not found on original Classical buildings. The gable roof of the pro-style porch forms a large pediment, although roofs are steeper than the Greek Revival form. Porch posts are thick and squat, usually resting on bases. Leaded glass, particularly in transoms and sidelights, are common. As in the Greek Revival, clapboard siding is the norm.

One hundred years after the county was first settled, architects and homeowners once again favored the Classical styles. Tools, materials, and building techniques had changed dramatically over the past generations: lumber, brick and nails were machine-processed and store-bought, glass was cheaply and readily available and no longer one of the most expensive materials in the house, closets and bathrooms were common, and houses were electrified, centrally heated, and often insulated. White paint inside and out indicated how weary homeowners were of dark Victorian woodwork. But no "modern" architectural style brought the county into the twentieth century. Rather, an era of revival styles brought about new Colonial, Federal, Saltbox, and Tudor houses, reinvented with new floor plans and conveniences.

America has gone through many revivals of Greek and Roman architecture in the past two hundred years. The 1876 Centennial and the 1893 Chicago Exposition reignited an interest in antiquity and neo-Classical (also referred to as Colonial Revival) architecture that continues to this day. Economic uncertainty and quickly-changing times made conservative revival styles popular with those longing for the security and familiarity of simpler times.

It was once thought that by the year 2000, we would be living underground in sunless houses resembling space pods. We forgot that millions of buildings would still be in place, and that the familiar will always have an attraction. The year 2000 is only five years away, but the most popular style for new domestic architecture is the Neo-Victorian—gingerbread, wrap-around porches, Palladian windows, and all.

Remsen merchant and postmaster A.P. Haight built his Classical Revival showplace behind his store in 1895. It was designed by Cleveland architect C.H. Hickox and featured many examples of modern technology, including electric burglar alarms. It had a slate roof and "twenty perch" (660 linear yards) of stone for the foundation and cellar. Large windows into the living or "front" room foreshadow the large picture windows popular in the twentieth century. Austere white paint, reminiscent of Classical styles, is usual for the exterior. The home's barren, robust exterior, while simple to the extreme to today's eyes, reflected the middle class solidity of an established citizen.

At the end of the nineteenth century, Wadsworth was the home of many important businesses, such as Ohio Match, Ohio Injector, and Ohio Salt. Many of the company officers built their homes in town. The B.F. Sonnastine residence, built in 1907 in the Classical Revival style, has paired Doric columns, a Palladian dormer window, porch railing and cresting, a second story porch, and a trabeated-arch doorway.

A view of Smith Road three miles east of Medina photographed by Liverpool Township photographer E.H. Raber at the end of the nineteenth century.

The National Register

Medina County Sites on the National Register of Historic Properties

Black River Viaduct, Baltimore and Ohio Railroad, Lodi.
Harrison G. Blake House. 314 East Washington Street, Medina.
Brunswick Town Hall and School. 1380 Pearl Road, Brunswick.
Burritt Blakeslee House. 3756 Fenn Road, Medina.
The Dague Farm. 5560 State Road, Sharon Township.
George Burr House. 740 Wooster Road, Lodi.
Matthew Chandler House. 6908 Ridge Road, Sharon Center.
Zimri Cook House. 6994 Spieth Road, Lester.
Charles Frank House and Store. Junction of State Route 23 and Ohio 303, Valley City.
Jacob Gayer House. 4508 Marks Road, Medina.
Halsey Hulburt House. 5484 Seville Road, Seville.
King-Phillips-Dieble House. 506 North Broadway, Medina.
Medina County Courthouse, Medina Square.
Medina County Public Square Historic District, Medina Square.
Judge Albert Munson House. 141 Prospect Street, Medina. (relocated)
Parmalee House. 1328 River Road, Valley City.
A.I. Root House. 662 West Liberty Street, Medina.
S.G. Barnard House. 221 West Libert Street, Medina (pending).
William Harrison Seymour House. 3306 South Weymouth Road, Weymouth.
Sharon Center Circle Historic District.
St. Mark's Episcopal Church. 146 College Street, Wadsworth.
St. Martin's Catholic Church. South of Valley City on Station Road.
St. Paul's Episcopal Church. 317 East Liberty Street, Medina.
Universalist Church of Westfield Center. Town Circle, Westfield Center.
York United Methodist Church. Norwalk Road, Mallet Creek.

This photo postcard was found in a local antique shop. Barely discernable under a magnifier are the words "A. Stearns 1881" on the barn's cupola. Both the 1874 and 1897 county maps reveal square dots indicating a house on Alijah Stearns' property just west of Brunswick Center on route 303. Perhaps Stearns replaced his Federal, Saltbox, Greek Revival, or even log house with this Classical Revival one. A leaded glass Palladian window fills the front facade pediment, the entryway has its own little pediment, an ashlar base supports the Doric-columned porch posts, and white paint gives the whole house what we now think of as Classical coloring.

Glossary

akroterion	decorations placed at the highest point of a building
anthemion	a design in the form of a stylized honeysuckle
architrave	the lowest part of the entablature (the beam resting directly on the columns), or the molding around a door or window
ashlar	hewn or cut stone laid in regular courses
balloon frame	a quick, inexpensive construction technique developed in mid-nineteenth century framed with light boards rather than hewn logs and nails rather than pegs
baluster	a post supporting a rail
barge board	see vergeboard
batten	a vertical strip of wood placed over a seam
bay window	a part of a building which projects from the main body and contains a window on each plane
belly window	a small, rectangular window in a frieze band
board and batten	siding comprised of vertical boards with battens covering the seams
bracket	an angled support projecting from a wall
capital	the topmost part of a column or pilaster
champfer	to remove the sharp corner edge of a post
clapboard	siding laid horizontally with the edges slightly overlapped against the elements
cornice	the projecting top of an entablature; where the wall meets the roof
crocket	a foliate projection used in Gothic architecture
dentils	small rectangular blocks forming a cornice
dormer window	a window projecting through a roof
eaves	the edge of a roof which projects over the building walls; the overhang
egg-and-dart	a pattern of alternating ovoids and arrows
ell	a small extension to the main part of a building
entablature	a horizontal band along the top of a wall consisting of an architrave, frieze and cornice
entasis	the slight swelling of a column shaft
facade	the front or main face of the building

Jacob Gish was born in Ohio in 1858. He built a Victorian farmhouse in 1874 on his Montville Township farm, still one of the county's finest.

fanlight	a semi-circular window; a lunette
finial	a decorative element reaching upward from the highest point of a building
fishscale shingles	wooden or slate shingles shaped and overlapped, resembling fishscales
fluting	vertical grooves cut along the shaft of a column
foliate	a leaf pattern
frame	made of timber
frieze	a horizontal band around the top of a building
gable	a triangular wall formed by the sloping planes of a roof; a roof with symmetrically sloping sides
gingerbread	ornate wooden trim popular during the Victorian era
grill	an open grating of wood or metal forming a screen
guttae	small, tear-shaped decorative elements
header	the short end of a brick
hewn	dressed; squared; cut
hip roof	a roof made of four sloping planes
hood molding	trim at the top of a window or door which is shaped to divert rain water
in antis	a small, inset porch, often supported by columns
Ionic	a Greek order utilizing a capital with volutes
jamb	the vertical pieces forming the sides of a window or door
keystone	the topmost stone or brick of an arch which holds the others in place
kneebrace	an angled piece of wood used as a bracket or brace
lancet	an opening which points at the top
lantern	an open structure at the top of a building allowing light and air to enter; a cupola or belvedere
lintel	the horizontal piece forming the top of a door or window
mansard roof	a very steep, almost vertical roof, generally pierced with dormers
masonry	made of brick or stone
metope	the square area between triglyphs in a Doric frieze
monitor	a building with a raised center area
mullion	the vertical strips between the lights of a window
oriel	a cantilevered bay window
Palladian window	a window flanked by two smaller windows and topped with a fanlight
pediment	a low-pitched gable at the front of a building or over a door or window
pendant	a hanging ornament
pilaster	an engaged column
pitch	the angle or slope of a roof
polychrome	many-colored
porte-cochere	a porch projecting over a driveway
portico	a roofed, columned porch
post-and-beam	construction supported by a log framework
pro-style	a projecting porch supported by columns
puncheon	a roughly dressed timber with one side hewed flat
quoin	one of the stones forming the corner of a building
respond	a pilaster or enagaged column supporting an arch
return	a short section of entablature at the top of a wall

ribbon window	a horizontal band of sashes
roundel	a round window
sash	a pane of glass set in a frame
shed roof	a roof which consists of one sloping plane
sidelight	a vertical row of windows flanking a door
spire	a steeple
stepped gable	the part of a wall which extends above the gable and and steps up symmetrically
stickwork	clapboarding placed in a variety of directions and positions to add interest to the surface of a building
stretcher	the long side of a brick
stringcourse	a slightly projecting horizontal masonry band
tetra-style	a projecting porch supported by four columns
timber frame	made of wood logs joined with pegs
trabeated arch	a doorway consisting of a door, transom, and sidelights, common in Greek Revival architecture
transom	a window overtop a door
triglyph	a rectangular block with two carved vertical grooves representing the end of a beam
truncated hip	a hip roof that does not form a peak
truss	a decorative strut in the topmost part of a gable
turret	a small tower projecting from a building
verandah	a large porch extending along one or more sides of a building
vergeboard	the edge that suspends over the gable end
vernacular	indigenous or native to a local area; naive
voisseur	one of the stones or bricks making up an arch
volute	a capital in the form of a scroll

Brunswick Center

Acknowledgments

We wish to dedicate this book to our families for their unceasing and gratefully appreciated support.

For valuable information, assistance, guidance, and advice, we are most grateful to Richard G. Clark, Peter R. King, Jeffrey A. Paolano, Jean Garwood, Cynthia S. Hagerman, Sean Blake, Andrew Borowiec, Earl L. Ertman, Jim Crowe, the Medina County Historical Society, the Western Reserve Historical Society, The Medina County *Gazette,* the Library of Congress, Judith Parrish, David Poling, Joe Warner, Theodore Blakeslee, Ross Trump, Marie Shurell, Janice Troutman Rains, The Summit County Historical Society, the Bierce Library of the University of Akron, John Gladden, John Miller of The University of Akron Archival Services, the Liverpool Township Historical Society, the Lodi Historical Society, Anita Weaver, the Seville Historical Society, LaVern Tolsma, Susan Batke, the Hinckley Historical Society, Andrew Phillips, Bob Hummel, the Sherwin-Williams Company, the A.I. Root Company, the Westfield Companies, the Westfield Historical Society, the Medina Library, the Hinckley Library, Ruth Ensworth, the Akron *Beacon Journal,* Mr. and Mrs. C. William Hower, Letha Ritter Waltz, the Ella M. Everhard Library in Wadsworth, Kate Dempsey, Dorothy Morris, Judith Schiff of the Yale University Alumni Archives, the Medina County Courthouse staff, Mr. and Mrs. David Fawcett, Henry Metzger, the Mattatuck Historical Society of Waterbury, Connecticut, Don Harvey, James Pahlau, the Sharon Heritage Society, Walter Thomas, the Medina Community Design Committee, the Department of Communications of The University of Akron, Dr. David Kyvig, the Granger Historical Society, Joseph G. Benes, John Heath, William Hromy, Dale Chase, Dr. Virginia Gunn, Harry Russell Clark, Sr., Bruce Weber, and a special thank you to Sean McKiernan.

Photo Credits

Photographs not listed were taken by the authors.

	Cover	Photograph by Kevin Olds
	Title page	Public Square, Medina, in 1846 from Howe's *History of Ohio*
5	Medina, 1868	Courtesy of the Medina County Historical Society
6	Medina in ashes	Courtesy of the Community Design Committee
	West side square	Courtesy of the Medina County Historical Society
7	South side square	Courtesy of the Medina County Historical Society
8	Homer family	From the collection of Susan McKiernan
9	County map	From the 1874 Medina County atlas
11	St. Paul's Cabin	From *The First One Hundred and Fifty Years of St. Paul's Episcopal Church, Medina, Ohio 1817-1967*
18	Rufus Ferris house	Photograph by Florence Phillips, courtesy of the Medina County Historical Society
	Burr house	Photograph by Don Harvey
20	Peter Moore house	Photograph by Florence Phillips, courtesy of the Medina County Historical Society
24	Franks house	Photograph by Florence Phillips, courtesy of the Medina County Historical Society
25	King house	Courtesy of the Medina County Historical Society
26	Hazen house	Photograph by Doug Garman, courtesy of The University of Akron Department of Communications
28	Benjamin drawing	From the collection of Susan McKiernan
31	Kennedy house	Photograph by Don Harvey
32	Sargent house	Photography by Florence Phillips, courtesy of the Medina County Historical Society
	Arnold house	Photograph by Don Harvey
33	Pierce house	Photograph by Don Harvey
	Pierce detail	Photograph by Don Harvey
35	Betz house	Photograph by Florence Phillips, courtesy of the Medina County Historical Society
36	Hammon house	Photograph by Florence Phillips, courtesy of the Medina County Historical Society
37	Hinckley house	From the collection of Susan McKiernan
39	Blakeslee house	Photograph by Florence Phillips, courtesy of the Medina County Historical Society
40	Walcott house	Photograph by Al Teufen
41	District school	Courtesy of the Medina County Historical Society
42	Octagon school	From *City of Wadsworth 1814-1989* by David Rodich
43	Northropville school	Courtesy of the Medina County Historical Society
	Lafayette school	Courtesy of the Lodi Historical Society
44	LeRoy school	Courtesy of the Westfield Historical Society
45	Lodi Academy	Courtesy of the Lodi Historical Society
	Weymouth school	From the collection of Susan McKiernan

46	Chippewa school	Courtesy of Brent and Bonnie Wilcox
	Mennonite Academy	From *City of Wadsworth 1814-1989* by David Rodich
48	Seymour house, old	Courtesy of Marie Shurell
	Seymour detail	Photograph by Doug Garman courtesy of The University of Akron Department of Communications
49	Brunswick church	Courtesy of the Medina County Historical Society
50	Sharon church	Photograph by Kevin Olds
	Wadsworth church	Courtesy of the Medina County Historical Society
51	Seville church	Courtesy of the Seville Historical Society
52	Weymouth church, 1937	Courtesy of the Western Reserve Historical Society
53	Congregational church	Courtesy of the Community Design Committee
55	St. Paul's church	Courtesy of the Medina County Historical Society
56	Abbeyville church	Photograph by Don Harvey
60	Lady with mower	From the collection of Susan McKiernan
61	Vine Street house	From the collection of Susan McKiernan
63	Gabarich house	Courtesy of the Liverpool Township Historical Society
64	South Court Street house	Photograph by Pat Bishop
	Reutter house	Photograph by E.H. Raber, courtesy of the Valley City Historical Society
65	Munson family	Courtesy of the Medina County Historical Society
66	Munson house	Courtesy of the Medina County Historical Society
	Munson store	Courtesy of the Medina County Historical Society
67	Barnard house	Photograph by Pat Bishop
	Levie Arnold house	Courtesy of the Medina County Historical Society
69	Bronson house	From the 1874 Medina County atlas
71	Homerville Town Hall	From the collection of Susan McKiernan
72	Courthouse	Drawing by Sean McKiernan
73	Medina Courthouse	Courtesy of the Medina County Historical Society
	Medina Square	Courtesy of the Medina County Historical Society
	First courthouse	Photograph by Florence Phillips, courtesy of the Medina County Historical Society
74	County infirmary	Courtesy of Brent and Bonnie Wilcox
	Depot	From the collection of Susan McKiernan
76	Gruninger plan	Courtesy of the Medina County Historical Society
78	Whiteside house	Photograph by Florence Phillips, courtesy of the Medina County Historical Society
	HABS detail drawing	Courtesy of the Western Reserve Historical Society
79	Ainsworth Lodge	Courtesy of the Medina County Historical Society
	Jason house	Courtesy of the Lodi Historical Society
80	Shepard house	Photograph by Pat Bishop
	Griesinger house	Photograph by Pat Bishop
81	Spitzer house	Photograph by Don Harvey
	Spitzer carriage house	Photograph by Pat Bishop
83	Stick square tower	Photograph by Pat Bishop
	Medina Stick house	Photograph by Don Harvey
84	Eastlake window	Photograph by Pat Bishop
85	Croft house	Photograph by Florence Phillips, courtesy of the Medina County Historical Society
	Burnham house	Photograph by Don Harvey
86	P.C. Parker house	Photograph by Pat Bishop
	P.C. Parker detail	Photograph by Pat Bishop
87	Albro house (top)	Photograph by Pat Bishop
89	Sipher house	Courtesy of the Medina County Historical Society
90	Reinhardt house	Photograph by Florence Phillips, courtesy of the Medina County Historical Society
92	Hardscrabble map	From the 1897 Medina County atlas
94	North Court detail	Photograph by Pat Bishop
95	Babcock house	Courtesy of the Sharon Heritage Society
	Brenner house	Photograph by Pat Bishop
96	McDowell plan	Courtesy of Andrew Phillips
	Mr. McDowell	Courtesy of the Medina County Historical Society
97	McDowell house	Photograph by Andrew Borowiec
	Palladian window	Drawing by Sean McKiernan
98	H.G. Blake, 1864	Courtesy of the Medina County Historical Society
99	Lomer Griffin	Courtesy of the Lodi Historical Society
100	The Giants	Courtesy of the Medina County Historical Society

102	Mallet Creek House	Courtesy of the Medina County Historical Society
104	Crawford house	Photograph by Florence Phillips, courtesy of the Medina County Historical Society
	Crawford detail	Photograph by Florence Phillips, courtesy of the Medina County Historical Society
106	Liverpool farm	Courtesy of the Liverpool Township Historical Society
	Hinckley ladies	Courtesy of the Hinckley Historical Society
115	Vargo barn	Courtesy of the Hinckley Historical Society
	Vargo raising	Courtesy of the Hinckley Historical Society
116	Tobacco farmers	Courtesy of the Medina County Historical Society
117	Weymouth bridge	From the collection of George Mason, courtesy of the Medina County Historical Society
118	Lodi bridge	Courtesy of Brent and Bonnie Wilcox
	Bridge supports	Courtesy of Brent and Bonnie Wilcox
	Trestle bridge	Courtesy of the Medina County Historical Society
119	Lodi scene	Courtesy of the Lodi Historical Society
120	Medina square, 1977	Photograph by Don Harvey
	Seville view, 1857	Courtesy of the Seville Historical Society
122	Bloomfield mill	Courtesy of Marie Shurell
	Spencer	From the collection of Susan McKiernan
	Wolcott building	Courtesy of the Lodi Historical Society
123	Tiernan store	Courtesy of Marie Shurell
	Crooks/Einhart store	Courtesy of Marie Shurell
	Weymouth view	From the collection of Susan McKiernan
124	American House	Courtesy of Brent and Bonnie Wilcox
	Hoppe factory	Courtesy of the Liverpool Township Historical Society
125	Phoenix building	Courtesy of the Medina County Historical Society
126	Seville general store	Courtesy of the Seville Historical Society
	Riley store	Courtesy of the Hinckley Historical Society
127	Muck farm	From the collection of Susan McKiernan
	Muck angels	Courtesy of the Lodi Historical Society
	Celery field	From the collection of Susan McKiernan
129	Chippewa dance hall	Courtesy of the Medina County Historical Society
	Chippewa hotel	Courtesy of the Medina County Historical Society
130	Hower building	Courtesy of the Lodi Historical Society
	Lodi street scene	Courtesy of the Lodi Historical Society
	Medina store	Photograph by Pat Bishop
131	Brenner hotel, old	Courtesy of Jim Cook
	Brenner hotel, current	Photograph by Pat Bishop
	Brenner doors	Photograph by Pat Bishop
132	Ohio Farmers' Greek shop	Courtesy of the Medina County Historical Society
133	Ohio Farmers'	Courtesy of the Westfield Historical Society
	Hawley house	Courtesy of Brent and Bonnie Wilcox
135	Rootville	Courtesy of Brent and Bonnie Wilcox
136	A.I. Root house	Courtesy of the A.I. Root Company
137	Brongers Greek house	Courtesy of the Hinckley Historical Society
138	Brongers family	Courtesy of the Hinckley Historical Society
	Bronger store, 1933	Courtesy of the Hinckley Historical Society
	Brongers house	Courtesy of the Hinckley Historical Society
139	Mr. Leach	Courtesy of the Medina County Historical Society
	Leach store	Courtesy of the Community Design Committee
140	Mr. and Mrs. Renz	Courtesy of the Medina County Historical Society
142	Haight house	Courtesy of the Granger Historical Society
	Sonnastine house	Courtesy of Brent and Bonnie Wilcox
143	Smith Road scene	Courtesy of the Liverpool Township Historical Society
144	Brunswick farm	From the collection of Susan McKiernan
145	Jacob Gish	From the 1874 Medina County atlas
	Gish farm	From the 1874 Medina County atlas
147	Brunswick, 1895	Courtesy of Brent and Bonnie Wilcox
153	S. Court scene	From the collection of Susan McKiernan
160	Weymouth Limited	From the collection of Susan McKiernan

Bibliography

A Backward Glance: Valley City and Liverpool Township 1810-1962, Valley City: Valley City Sesquicentennial, Inc., 1962.
An Outline History of Brunswick 1815-1965. Brunswick: Historical Committee of the Brunswick Sesquicentennial, 1965.
Atlas and Directory of Medina County, Ohio. Cleveland: The American Atlas Company, 1897.

Baker, Jerald. *History of Religion in Medina County*, 1976.
Baldwin, James. *The First One Hundred and Fifty Years of St. Paul's Episcopal Church, Medina, Ohio 1817-1967*.
Beecher, Catherine and Harriet Beecher Stowe. *American Woman's Home*. New York: J.B. Ford and Co., 1869.
Benjamin, Asher. *The American Builder's Companion; or, a system of architecture particularly adapted to the present style of building*, sixth edition. Boston: R.P. and C. Williams, 1827.
_____, *The Practical House Carpenter*. Boston: Arthur, R.P. and C. Williams and Annin and Smith, 1830.
_____, *The Architect, or Complete Builder's Guide*. Boston: Benjamin B. Mussey, 1845.
B.H. Wood Company ledger, Medina, Ohio: 1882-1883.
Borukva, Jo Ann. *Highland Heritage*, self published, 1986.
Brouse, Donald. *A Trip to Spencer 1823-1973*. Spencer, Ohio: Sesquicentennial Book Committee, 1973.
Brown, Edward, A.M. *Wadsworth Memorial*. Wadsworth: Steam Printing House, 1875.
Bushman, Richard L., *The Refinement of America: Persons: Houses: Cities*. New York: Alfred A. Knopf, 1992.
Business Directory of Wayne and Medina Counties, 1897.

Cavin, Lee. "There Were Giants on the Earth". Seville: the Seville Chronicle, 1959.
Cherry, P.P. *Western Reserve and Early Ohio*. Akron: R.L. Fouse, 1921.
Clark, Clifford Edward. Jr. *The American Family Home, 1800-1960*. Chapel Hill: The University of North Carolina Press, 1986.
Cole, Jane. "Forty-one Years of Factory Life". Personal account of work experience at A.I. Root Company 1870-1911.
Combination Atlas of Medina County, Ohio. Chicago: L.H. Evers, 1874.
Condit, Carl W. *American Building: Materials and Techniques from the Beginning of the Colonial Settlements to the Present*. Chicago: University of Chicago Press, 1982.
Condon, George E. and Willard Largent. *History of Ohio Farmers' Insurance Company*, Willard: R.R. Donnelly and Sons, n.d.
Cornelius, Mrs. *The Young Housekeeper's Friend*. Boston: Brown, Taggard and Chase, 1859.
_____, *The Corner Cupboard or, Facts for Everybody*. New York: Dick and Fitzgerald, 1859.

Deming, Moses. *Autobiography, 1777-1868*.
The Democratic Whig, February 2, 1848.
Donaghy, Elisabeth. *At Home: The American Family 1750-1870*. New York: Harry Abrams, 1990.
Duff, William A. *History of North Central Ohio, Embracing Richland, Ashland, Wayne, Medina, Lorain, Huron and Knox Counties*. 2 vol. Topeka: Historical Publishing Company, 1931.

Ensworth, Ruth and Helen Vaughn. *Early Sharon Township*, self published, 1981.

Foley, Mary Mix. *The American House*. New York: Harper Colophon Books, Harper and Row, 1980.
Frary, I.T. *Early Homes of Ohio*. New York: Dover Publications, 1970.
_____, *Ohio in Homespun and Calico*. Richmond: Garrett and Massie, 1942.

Giles, John F. Medina County map. Philadelphia: Matthews and Taintor, 1857.
Goldsmith, Rev. G. *A Grammar of General Geography*, new edition. London: c. 1864.
Goodrich, Charles A. *A History of the United States*. Hartford: H. F. Sumner and Company, 1833.
_____, *Great Events in the History of North and South America*. Hartford: House and Brown, 1849.
Gramley, Allene Holt. *The World's Tallest Couple (The Love Giants)*, Mansfield: Appleseed Press, 1983.
Guthrie, William. *A Universal Geography; or, a view of the present state of the known world*. Philadelphia: Benjamin Warner, 1820.

Handlin, David P. *The American Home: Architecture and Society, 1913-1915*. Boston: Little, Brown and Co., 1979.
Hange, Mark et al., *Exploring Barns of Medina County*. Medina: Historical Projects of Medina County, Inc., 1987.
Hartley, Dorothy. *Lost Country Life*. New York: Pantheon Books, 1979.

Hatcher, Harlan. *The Western Reserve: The Story of New Connecticut in Ohio*. New York: The Bobbs-Merrill Co. Inc., 1949.
Hawke, David Freeman. *Nuts and Bolts of the Past: A History of American Technology, 1776-1860*. New York: Harper and Row, 1988.
Hinckley Township 1825-1975. Sesquicentennial Book Committee, 1975.
Historic American Buildings Survey. Washington, D.C.: Department of the Interior, 1934.
History of Homer Township. Compiled and written by Homer School Students. Medina: The Medina County *Gazette*, 1946.
History of Medina County and Ohio. Chicago: Baskin and Battey, 1881.
Hosmer, Henry. *Notes on the History of Seville*.
Howard, Hugh. *How Old is this House?* New York: Noonday Press, 1989.
Howe, Henry. *Historical Collections of Ohio*. Columbus, State of Ohio, 1902.
Hutslar, Donald A. *Log Construction in the Ohio Country 1750-1850*. Columbus: Ohio University Press, 1992.
_____, "The Ohio Farmstead: Farm Buildings as Cultural Artifacts" *Ohio History* (Summer 1981): p. 221-237.

Kilbourn, John. *The Ohio Gazetteer, or Topographical Dictionary*. Columbus: Scott and Wright, 1833.

Lacour-Gayet, Robert. *Everyday Life in the United States before the Civil War 1830-1860*. New York: Frederick Ungar Publishing Co., 1969.
Larkin, Jack. *The Reshaping of Everyday Life 1790-1840*. New York: Harper and Row, 1988.
Lieber, Francis, ed. *Encyclopaedia Americana*. Phildelphia: Carey and Lea, 1831.
Longdon, William Chauncy. *Everyday Things in American Life 1776-1876*. New York: Chas. Schribner's Sons, 1941.

Marston, James. *American Building: The Historical Forces that Shaped It*. Boston: Houghton Mifflen Company, 1966.
Martinson, Earl, chairman, Historical Committee. *Lodi Sesquicentennial 1811-1961*, self published, 1961.
McAlester, Virginia and Lee. *A Field Guide to American Houses*. New York: Alfred A. Knopf, 1984.
McClelland, Pauline Griesinger oral history interview.
McMurry, Sally. *Families and Farmhouses in 19th Century America: Vernacular Design and Social Change*. New York: Oxford University Press, 1988.
Medina County Genealogical Society. *Tombstone Inscriptions From the Cemeteries in Medina County, Ohio*. Evansville, Ind.: Whipporwill Publications, 1984.
Medina County Historical Society. *History of Medina County*. Medina, 1948.
"Medina County Up To Date", The Medina *Sentinel*, c. 1912.
The Medina County *Gazette*. Medina: 1870 to 1900.
The Medina *Democrat*, 1838.
The Medina *Examiner*, August 27, 1856.
Morse, Jedidiah, D.D. *The American Universal Geography, 7th edition*. Charlestown: Lincoln and Edmands, 1819.
Murray, Zola F. *Seville, Ohio 1816-1941*, Wadsworth: Banner Press, 1941.

Noble, Allen. *Wood, Brick and Stone: The North American Settlement Landscape*. Amherst: The University of Massachusetts Press, 1984.
Northrop, N.B. *Pioneer History of Medina County*. Medina: George Redway, publisher, 1861.
_____, *Autobiography 1791-1867*.

Ohio *Free Press*, July 2, 1836.
Ohio Historic Inventory Forms for Medina County and Wadsworth City, 1979.
One Hundred Years of the First Congregational Church of Weymouth, Ohio 1835-1935.
An Outline History of Brunswick 1815-1965. Brunswick Susqui-centennial Committee, Inc., 1965.
Overman, William D. *Ohio Town Names*. Akron, 1958.

Phillips, Florence and Mrs. Clark Reinhardt. "Our Life in the Big House, personal account of the King-Phillips-Deible House, Medina 1895-1917".
Pitcher, Barbara Welton. "Welton, A Street, A Ditch, An Ancestor". *The Colorado Genealogist*, vol. 51, no. 2, May, 1990, pp. 31-37.
Promey, Vesta Welton, compiler. Welton family genealogy.

Rodich, David. *City of Wadsworth 1814-1989*. Wadsworth: Banner Printing Company, 1989.
Root, Amos I. *The ABC and XYZ of Bee Culture*, 5th edition. Medina: A.I. Root Bee Library, 1948.
_____, *An Eyewitness Account of Early American Beekeeping: The Autobiography of A.I. Root*, Medina: The A.I. Root Co., 1984.
Roth, Leland M. *A Concise History of American Architecture*. New York: Harper and Row, 1979.
Rufner, Jessie Jason, compiler. "History of Harrisville Township". Medina: Medina County *Gazette*, 1946.

Schapiro, Eleanor Iler, editor. *Historical Highlights of Medina*, complied by the students of the Medina High School class of 1966. Medina: Alfred Meyers Lithographers, Inc., 1966.
_____, *Wadsworth: Center to City*. Wadsworth: *Banner* Press, 1938.
_____, *Wadsworth Heritage*. Wadsworth: *News Banner*, 1964.
Selders, H. *Home Coming and Centennial Souvenir*. Lodi: Cunningham and Dunlap, 1911.
Seville 1816-1916, the evolution of a rural community, 1916.
Sloan, Eric. *An Age of Barns*. New York: Ballantine Books, 1975.
_____, *Sketches of America Past*. New York: Promontory Press, 1986.
Stilgoe, John R. *Borderland: Origins of the American Suburb, 1820-1939*. New Haven: Yale University Press, 1988.
Stoll, Hazel and Willis. *History of Remsen Corners, Granger Township*, 1988.
The Story of Litchfield, Ohio 1831-1981. Litchfield: Litchfield Historical Society, 1981.
Sutherland, Daniel E. *The Expansion of Everyday Life 1860-1876*. New York: Harper and Row, 1989.
Swigart, Mrs. John. *Sharon Township: From Forest to Farms*, 1938.

Thomas, Evelyn, compiler. "Medina County Landmarks". Medina, Medina County *Gazette*.
Thomas, John J. *Farm Implements, and the Principles of their Construction and Use*. New York: Harper and Brothers, 1855.
"Thriving Medina 1898" Medina: Medina County *Gazette* issue featuring Medina businesses.

Upton, Harriet Taylor. *History of the Western Reserve*. Chicago: The Lewis Publishing Company, 1910.

Valley City and Liverpool Township Commerative Book. Valley City: Valley City Sesquicentennial Committee, Inc., 1962.
Vereb, Elaine Taylor. "Medina in the Civil War", 1986.

Walker, Lester. *American Shelter: An Illustrated Encyclopedia of the American House*. Woodstock, New York: Overlook Press, 1981.

Young, Andrew W. *First Lesson in Civil Government: A Comprehensive View of the Government of the State of Ohio*. Cleveland: M. C. Younglove, 1848.

Index

Numbers in **boldface** type refer to illustrations.

Abbeyville, **56**
Acme, 92
Adam, James and Robert, 15
Agard, Benjamin, 22
agriculture/crops, 8, 11, 22- 24, 31, 41, 110, 114, 120, 127
Ainsworth Lodge, **79**, 122
A.I. Root Company, 9, 101, 120, **134**, 135
Akron, 9, 20, 25, 32, 76, 99, 119
Albro, W.H., 87
Alger, Russell, 100
Allen, P.T., 69
Amish, 103
Andrews, Ed, 9
apartments/multiple family housing, **6**, 17, **61**, 95, 126
architects, 15, 23, 28, 39, 46, 49, 51, 55- 56, 59, 76, 78, 87, 93, 102, 128, 142
architecture, 5, 8-9, 102
    Classical, 16, 19, 23, 28-29, **47**, 49, 51, 80, 89, 96, 137, 140, 142
    Classical Revival, 5-6, **31, 74, 135**, 137, **138, 140-142, 144**
    Colonial farmhouse, 14, 21, **22**, 23
    Eastlake, **59**, 80, **84-87**, 121, **136, 158**
    False front, **128, 147**
    Federal, **5, 6, 15-20**, 23, 30, 33, **37**, 49, **50-51**, 62, 70, **72-73, 78, 121**, 124, **125**, 141
    Georgian, 14
    Gothic Revival, **47-49, 53-56, 58**, 59, 62, **77-78**, 80, 105, 107, **102- 105, 109, 111**, 120, **133, 142**
    Greek Revival, 5-6, 15-16, 19, 21, **23, 40–43, 45**, 47, 49, **50-52**, 55-56, **58**, 62- 63, **77, 103-104, 123**, 126, **132**, 137
    Italianate, **6-7, 63, 67**, 69, **76-77, 79, 82**, 88, 100, 102, 105, **120, 121, 130, 139-140**
    Monitor, 40
    New England Large, **14, 22**
    Queen Anne, 83, **84, 88-90**, 93, 94, 107, 121, **133, 134, 136**, 140, 142
    Renaissance Revival, **158**
    Richardsonian Romanesque, 76, 93, **128**
    Saltbox, **21-22**, 23, **32**, 142
    Second Empire, **44-45, 68**, 69, 71, **73**, 84, 102, **131**
    Shingle Style, 93, **94-95**, 96, **97**, 121
    Shotgun, 102
    Stick Style, **43, 49, 71**, 74, **80-83**, 107, **129, 139**
    Tuscan, 63, 77, **79**
    vernacular, 5, 14, **41**, 46, 52, **102-106, 145**
    Victorian, 9, 18, 32, **46**-47, 49, 51, **53-55, 61-69**, 73, **75**, 80, 88, **89**, 105, **108, 120, 133, 139**, 141
    Western Reserve, **35-40**, 47, **126**
Arnold, Mrs. Levie, **67**

asheries, 8, 119
Austin, Ben, 132

Babcock, Effie, 95
Badger, Austin, 70
Bagdad, 14, 23, 53, 115
Baker, O.T., 28
Baldwin family, 86
Baldwin Wallace College, 99, 100
balloon frame construction, 60, 63, 80, 137
Barnard, S.G., 67
barns, 5, 10, 16, 18, 20-21, 23, 27, **47**, 49, 63, 93, 102, 107-108, **109**, 110, **111-116**, 132, **144**
Bates, Anna Swan, **100**-101
Bates, Captain Martin V., **100**-101
Beebetown, 92
Beech, Henry, 101
Beecher, Catherine, 60
Benjamin, Asher, 23, 28, 39
Behr, William, 137
Betz, Carl, 35
Bishop, A.B., 55
Blake, Harrison G., 27, 65, **98**, 125, 132
Blakeslee, Burritt, 39, 102
blinds/shutters, 23, 37, 39, 61, 64, 82
Boardman, Elijah, 7-8, 18, 57, 70
Bogus Hollow, 91
Boneta, 91
Bostwick Brothers, 116
Bowen, William, 101
Boyden, A.L. 135
Brader, F.A., 109
Brenner, Ephriam, 76, 95, 131, 140
bridges, **117-118**
Brongers, John, 14, 126, 137, **138**
Bronson, Hiram, 55, 69
Brunswick Township, 8-9, 18, **49**, 102
Brunswick Village, 8-9, **49**, 119, **144, 147**
Buchtel College/The University of Akron, 5, 99
builders, contractors, 15-17, 23, 28-29, 32, 34, 36, 38-39, 50, 52, 62-63, 76, 80, 84, 87, 96, 102, 104
Burnham, Nell and Nelson, 84
Burr, George, 16, 18
Burr, Russell, Jr., 15, 16
Butler, Phineas, 15

Camp, Charles, 114
canal, 60, 120
Cannon, Ida, 130
Carpenter, Judge J.S., 98
carpenters/joiners/builders, 15-17, 23, 28-29, 32, 34, 36, 38-39, 50, 52, 54, 62-63, 76, 80, 84, 96, 102, 104
Carr, Nathan, 56
cemeteries, 5, 9, 57, **58**, 59, 62, 70

154

Mound Hill, 7, 57, 101
Spring Grove, 57, **59**, 76
Woodlawn, Lodi, 57, **58**
Woodlawn, Wadsworth, 57
Chatham, 21, 41, **51**, 54, **62, 79**, 110
Chatham Township, 8, **21, 39, 79**, 91, 112, **113**
Cherry, Austin and P.P., 98, 99
Chippewa Lake, 7, 9, **46,** 129
Chippewa Lake Park, 9, **129**
churches/religions, 5, 10-11, 18, 27, 41-**42**, 46-47, **49**, 50-**56,** 57, 62, 75, 99, 101, 135
    Abbeyville Zion Lutheran, **56**
    Baptist, 63, 101
    Brunswick Disciples, **49**
    Catholic, **56**
    Chatham Congregational, **51,** 54
    Chatham Methodist, **54**
    Congregational, 10, 11, **52,** 50-**54,** 57, 71, 134
    Disciples, **49, 52, 146**
    East Granger, **52**
    East Homer, **54**
    Emmanuel, **53**
    Lutherans, 50, 54, **56**
    Medina Congregational, 10-11, 50, 52, **53**, 57
    Mennonite, 46, **50**
    Methodist, 12, **54-55**
    Quakers, 91
    Remsen, **53**
    Seville Presbyterian, **51**
    Sharon Universalist, **50**
    St. Mark's, **50**
    St. Martin of Tours, **56**, 107
    St. Mary's, **55**
    St. Paul's Episcopal, **11**, 49, **55**, 57, 76
    United Church of Christ, **53-55**
    Valley City Lutheran, 50
    Wadsworth Reformed, **42**
    Weymouth, 50- **52**
    York United Methodist, **55**
Civil War, 8-9, 23, 35-36, 40, 47, 49-50, 52-53, 57, 59- 61, 63, 66, 75, 80, 84, 96, 99-100, 106, 110, 120, 125, 137
Clark, D.P., 87
Clark, John, 120
Clark, William P., 41
Cleaveland/Cleveland, 5, 8-10, 14-15, 56, 69, 85, 98, 117, 119-120, 134, 137, 142
coal, 9, 30, 61, 69, 71, 102, 120-121
Coit, H.H., 91
Collier, George, 132
colors/paint, 5, 14-15, 19, 22-23, 35-37, 41-43, 47, 51, 53, 56, 60-64, 67-68, 70, 80, 87-88, 93-94, 144

commercial buildings, 2-3, **5-7, 24, 66, 119-134, 139-140,** 147
commercial ventures, 5, 8-9, 23, 25-27, 30, 33, 35, 40, 60, 65, 78, 80, 82, 90-91, 96, 102, 121, 124-125, 127, 132, 134, 137, 139-140
communication, 25, 60
Community Design Center, 65, 66
Connecticut, 7-8, 12, 14, 18, 22, 39, 49, 69-70, 91, 98
Connecticut Land Company, 7, 25, 129
construction methods, 10, 15, 20, 23, 29, 47, 63, 60, 63, 80, 84, 88, 93, 110, 122
Cook, Frances E., 43
Cook, George, 51
Cook, Zimri, 77
Coolman, John, 10
Courthouse, Medina County, 6, 41, 70, **72-73**, 98
Crawford homestead, **104**
Croft, Dr. W.B., 85
Culley, John L., 58
Culver, E.R., 107

dairy industry, 9, 112
Deible, Edward H., 25
depots, **74**, 92, 124
Doane, Timothy, 23, 50, 52, 70, 119, 122
Downing, Andrew Jackson, 47

Eastlake, Charles Locke, 59, 84
Easton, Thomas, 100
economic conditions, 5, 8, 60, 106, 110, 119-121
education, 41, 43, 46-47, 49, 60, 67, 71, 98, 100, 107, 119-120
Edwards, Charles and Susie, **48**
electricity, 25, 60, 61, 87-88, 134-135, 142
England, 7, 10-11, 14, 16, 21, 23, 32, 51, 84, 88, 98-100, 118, 124
Erhart, 92
Esselburn's Corners, 91

Fahrion, E., 114
farm animals, 8, 10, 23, 110
farmhouse, **8**, 11, **14-15, 17,** 21, **23**, 26, **29-40**, 43, 47, **48,** 60-61, **63, 64, 67-69, 77, 82, 85, 103, 106-109, 144-145**
farms, 5- 7, 9-11, 14, 30, 39, 42, 57, 60-61, 68, 85, 91, 93, 99-101, 106-**107, 109, 127, 144-145**
Ferris, Rufus, 10, 18
fire of 1848, 9, 71, 98
fire of 1870, 5, **6**, 9, 60, 63, 71, 76, 102, 120-121, 124-125, 130-131
fires, 5-6, 9-10, 35, 39, 54, 60, 63, 70-71, 104, 106, 132
Fitch, Luther, 31
Fixler's Corners, 91

155

Fleming, Walter, 51
Ford, Mary, 54
forests, 7-8, 10-11, 15-16, 49, 60, 70, 93, 110, 119
Fowler, James, 129
Fowler, Samuel, 91
Fowler, Orson Squire, 77
frame construction, 10, 15, 18, 20, 22, 47
Frank, John, 42
Franks, Charles, 24
Frary, I.T., 39
Freese, John, 70
Fugitive Slave Act, 27, 98

Gargett, John, 32
Garden Isle Farm, **127**
Germany, 8, 10-11, 13, 24, 46, 49-50, 53-57, 81, 89, 91, 102, 110, 124
Gibb, Horace and Milo, 121
"gingerbread" trim, 18, **46**-47, **53, 62, 69, 82, 104, 108, 126**
Gish farmstead, **145**
Gish, Jacob, **145**
glass/windows, 10-11, 14-15, 17-19, 23, 25-26, 28, 32, 37, 39, 41-42, 47, 49, 50-51, 53- 56, 60-61, 63, 67-69, 75, 79, 81, 84, 87, 89, 94, 126, 142
Gleanings in Bee Culture, 120, 134-135
Granger Township, 8, **26, 38**, 41, **52,** 91, **103, 141**
Gridley, Orrin, 39
Griesinger, C.L., 27, 80
Griffin, Chedom Lomer, **99**
Groll, John, 119
Gruninger Company, 59, 71, 74, 76, 80, 90, 96, 128, 131-132
Guilford Township, 8-10, **18-19**, 23, 65, **75, 78, 89-90,** 91, 98, 100-101, **104**, 116

Haight, A.P., 142
Haldo, 91, 127
Hammerschmidt family, 86
Hard, Abraham II and Rebecca, 12
Hardscrabble, 91
hardware/nails, 10-11, 15, 23, 47, 60, 63, 65, 70, 87, 107, 142
Harris, Joseph, 8, 70
Harrisville Township, 7-8, **13, 15, 16, 18, 29,** 57, **58,** 70, 72, 79, 104, **116**-117, **118, 119, 122, 127, 130**
Hawley, A.G., 44, 132
Hawley, A.H. and Frank, 132
Hazel and Bennet Store, **128**
Hazen, George, 26
Heacox, Charles, 87
health, 42, 70, 72, 74, 77, 83, 95, 100-101, 120, 122, 127, 139
heating/stoves/fireplaces, 10-11, 14, 17-18, 23, 24, 45-47, 60-61, 63, **65,** 69, 79-81, 86, 88, 96, 99-100, 103, **106**, 134
Henry, Joe, 31
Hickox, C.H., 104
Hickox, James S., 65
Hickox, William, 71
Hinckley Center, 14, 41, **58,** 101, 117, 119, **126, 137-138**
Hinckley Ridge, 91
Hinckley, Samuel, 8
Hinckley Township, 8, 14, **32, 37, 58,** 91-92, 99-100, 102, **106, 115, 137-138**
Hinsdale, Albert, 10
Hinsdale, George, 50
historic inventory of Medina County architecture, 5, 79
Historic American Buildings Survey, 50, **52,** 78
Holcomb, Ashabel, 64
Holcomb, J.R., 20
Hollow Ware Foundry, 9, 86, 100-101, 120
Holmes, Judge, 8
Homerville, 8, **71, 82,** 93
Homer Township, **8,** 10-11, **13, 26,** 29, **54,** 57, **71, 82, 103,** 114, **158**
Hoppe, Charles, 124
Horr Warner Company, **127**
Hosmer, Henry, 10, 78
hospitals, 71-72, 74, **79**
hotels, **119, 124, 131**
Hower Store, 139
Hudson, David, 20
Hudson, Dr., 57
Hulbert, Halsey, 24
Hunsberger, Ephriam, 46, 82

industrialization, 9, 47, 49, 60-61, 63, 67-68, 80, 93, 142
inns, 19, **24, 32,** 70, **121**
interior scenes, **65, 106, 138**
inventors, Medina County, 98, 101, 134

jails, 70, 71, 100
Jarvis, Calvin, 18
Jason, George W., 72, 79

Katytown, 91, 99
Kelly, Patrick, 56
Kennedy, John, 31
Kent, Aaron, 46
King, David, 25
King, Leister, 25
King, Tom, 57
King-Phillips-Deibel House, 25
Kinney, O.S., 45

Lafayette, **43,** 91
Lafayette Township, 8, **43, 46, 67,** 71, **74,** 91, 100, **129**
Lampson, Richard, 54, 121

lanterns/cupolas, **42, 46,** 70, **71, 77-79, 81, 144**
Leach, Frank, **139**
Leach, O.N. and Electa, 139
Lefever, Minard, 23
LeRoy Center, 41, **44,** 55, **89,** 91, **132, 133**
Lester, 33, **77**
Lewis, Gertie, 99
libraries, 9, 25, 71
lighting, 10-11, 25, 41, 46, 60-61, 65, 78, 90, 96, 102, 116, 126, 128, 133
Lincoln, Abraham, 57, 98
Lindsley, Benjamin, 70
Litchfield, **58,** 63, 71, **75,** 91
Litchfield Town Hall, 71, **75**
Litchfield Township, 8, **59,** 63, **75,** 114
literary societies, 9, 71
Liverpool Township, 7-8, **17-18, 21, 24, 32, 35-36, 42, 53, 56-** 57, 62, **63, 64, 76,** 91, 102, **105-106,** 116, 119, 140
livestock/animals, 8, 10, 70-71, 79, 99, 101, 106, 114, 117, 119, 130, 137
Lloyd, Gordon W., 55
Lodi/Harrisville Reserve, 9, **15-16, 18,** 41, **45,** 57- **58,** 70-71, 72, **79,** 91, 99, **104,** 119, **122,** 130
log structures, 5- 6, 8–10, **11-13,** 14-16, 18, 21, **22,** 23, 31, 33-34, 41, 47, 49, 53- 56, 70, 106, 109-110, 134
Loomis, Julia, 15
Lorain County, 8, 28, 54, 99, 139
Low, Benjamin, 52
Lowe, George, 133
Loveland, Mrs. R.P., 117

Mallet Creek, **33,** 55, **65,** 102, **121**
Mansard roof, **44, 45, 68-69, 72-73, 131, 133**
Martin, J.W., 80
Marysville, 17, 62, 91
masonry, 5-6, 9, 15, 17-18, 20, 23-24, 26, 30- 32, 36, 40, 45-49, 55-56, 59-60, 63, 68, 70-71, 76, 78, 82, 84, 86, 96, 102-103, 108, 118, 128, 132, 138
materials, building, 10-11, 23, 47, 60, 63, 93-94, 102, 117, 142
Matteson, H., 90
McClelland, Pauline Griesinger, 27
McDowell, Elizabeth Blake, 27
McDowell family, 27
McDowell, Robert M., **96**
McGregor, John, 42
McKinley, William, 65, 100
Mecca, 70, 91
Medina City/Village, **2-3, 5-7-** 9, 15, **18, 20,** 25, 27, **32**-33, 41, 46, **53, 55,** 57, **59, 61, 62, 64,** 65, **66-67, 68,** 69, 71, **73,** 80, **81, 83-90, 94-95, 96, 97,** 98, 99, 110, **120,** 124-**125,** 128, 130-131, 134-136, 139-140, **153**
Medina County atlases, 5, 42, 144

Medina County Courthouse, 6, 41, 70, **72-73,** 98
Medina County **Gazette,** 5, **7,** 57, 60, 64, 74, 76, 86-87, 96, 98-99, 118, **120,** 121, **128,** 130, 133
Medina County Historical Society, 13, 65, 67, 71, **86**
Medina County history, 7-9
Medina County Infirmary, 57, 71, **74,** 98
Medina Square, **2- 3, 5-7,** 8-9, 25, 59-60, 65, 72, **73,** 102, **120,** 124, 134, **153**
Medina Township, 7-8, **11, 14,** 25, **31, 38-39, 43,** 51-**52,** 55, 57, 114, **117**
meeting houses, 11, 12, 18, 41, 49-50, 52, 70-71
Miller, Hiram, 99
Miller, Jacob, 15, 17
mills, 10, 13-15, 22-23, 27, 33, 40, 49, 63, 80, 105, 119, **122**
Montville Township, 8, 25, 57, 59, **107, 118, 145**
Moore, Peter A., 20, 32, 91
mortgages, 60
muck farms, 9, **127**
Munson, Albert/Cora/Lyman, **65,** 66, 91

National Register Properties, **18, 24-25, 27, 36, 47-48, 50, 55-56, 66-67, 72-73, 77, 118, 136,** 143
Native Americans, 7, 57, 98, 119
Nettleton, Albert, 90
Nettleton, George, 96
New England, 8, 10, 14, 21, 33, 37, 41, 47, 49-51, 70, 93, 98
Newcomer farm, 43
Newton homestead, 82
New York State, 7, 15
North, C.P., 75
Northrop, Joseph, 43
Northrop, Morris, 118
Northrop, N.B., 10, 43, 110
Northropville, **43**
Northwest Ordinance, 7
Northwest Territory, 7

Octagon buildings, **42,** 53, 77, 79, 90, 94, **116**
Ohio Farmers' Insurance Company, 24, 40, 44, 55, 91, **132-133**
Ohio **Free Press,** 120
Ohio Historic Inventory, 5, 142
Ohio Injector Company, 9, 142
Ohio Match Company, 9, 72, 120, 142
Ohio Salt Company, 9, 120, 142
Olcutt, Charles, 98
Old Phoenix Bank, **6-7,** 76, 96, 98, 121, **125,** 135, **139**
outbuildings, 10, 21, 23, 41, 43, 71, **81, 84,** 106, 108-110, 112, **139**

Packard, George, 21
Pardee, George, 57
Parker, Paul C., 86, 117

parks, **7**, 9, 57, 62, 70, **73, 129,** 137
parlor, 38, 47-48, **65**, 86, 88, **106**-107
Parmalee, D., 105
Parsons, Moses, 54
Pawnee, 91
Pennsylvania, 7- 8, 14, 23, 46, 69, 109-110
"Pennsylvania Dutch", 13, 50, 110
Perkins, Simon, 20, 32
Phillips, Fremont, 25
Pierce, Thompson, 33
pioneer history, 7-8, 10-11, 14, 18, 22, 27, 37, 41, 50, 59-60, 69, 99, 106, 110
plumbing, 25, 60, 68, 81, 87, 96, 133, 134
political history, 9, 11, 25, 27, 56, 65, 69, 82, 98, 100-101, 120, 132
Portage County, 7, 70
post and beam construction, 10, 23
Potter's Pinnacle, 91
Prentice, Barney, 20
prices/costs, 13-4, 21, 24, 26, 31-33, 41, 43-47, 50-55, 58-59, 68, 70-72, 74, 77, 79-80, 86-87, 95-96, 99-100, 104, 110, 112, 126, 134, 136
public buildings, 5, **7-8**, 68, 70, **71-75,** 120, 141-146

Raber, E.H., 64
railroads, 9, 60, 69, **74**, 91-92, 102, 106, 120, 124
Reinhardt, G.W., 90
Remsen, 8, 52, **53**, 91, **142**
Renz, John and Barbara, 76, **140**
Rettig, John, 140
Reutter, Charles, 117
Reutter family, 64
Reyser family, **8**
Rhoades, Jesse, 98
Richards, Robert Usher and Steward, 119
Richardson, Henry Hobson, 93, 128
Richert, David, 110
Riley, Ramson and Wallace, 126
Risley, 91
Ritter, A.E. and Thelma Ritter Waltz, 107
River Styx, 10, 65, **75**, 91
roads, 7-9,27, 30, 33-36, 41-43,45, 54- 55, 57, 59, **60,** 65-66, 70-71, 83, 86, 90-91, 96, 106, 117-118, 134-135
Robertson, David, 55
Rogers, Thomas, 54
Rohn, Daniel, 109
Root, A.I., 9, 101, 120-121, 136
Root, Connie/Ernest/Huber, 135
Root, Susan Hall, 134, 136
"Rootville", 134, **135**

Salt Spring Town, 91, 119
Sargent and Peak, 70
Sargent family, 32

Sausaman, William, 40
sawmills, 10, 13-15, 22-23, 33, 49, 63, **122**
Schneibley, Rudulphus, 13
schools, 5, 11, **41-46**, 70, 102
    Chippewa Lake, **46**
    District School on State Road, **41**
    Frank, **42**
    Lafayette Township #10, **43**
    LeRoy school, **44**
    Liverpool Township, **76**
    Lodi, 45
    Medina High School, 41
    Mennonite, **46**, 82
    Newcomer, **43**
    Northropville, **43**
    octagon, **42**
    Wadsworth academy, **42**
    Weymouth, **45,** 52
    Wright, **43**

Shallow, machine-carved Eastlake detailing adorns this one-over-one sash Renaissance Revival window in Homer Township.

settlement of Medina County, 5, 7-8, 10-11, 14, 16-18, 22, 33, 37, 41, 43, 59, 59-60, 69, 99, 106, 110
Seville, 7, 9, **18-19**, 41, **51**, 57, 71, **78, 89-90**, 98, 100-101, **120, 126**
Seymour, Lathrop, 23, 45, 52, 57, 119, 122
Seymour, William Harrison, 47-48, 61- 62, 119
Shane, S.J., 110
Sharon Center, **31**, 41, **50, 69, 91, 95, 99, 121**
Sharon Township, 8, **20**, 31-32, 50, **95**, 98, **103, 121**
Shaw, Richard Norman, 88
Shepard, O.C., 27, 80
Showalter, Christian, 46
Silver Creek, **30**
Simmons, Dr. A.L., 30
Simmons family, 28
Simmons, Jonathan, 30, 132
Sipher family, 61, 69, 89, 139
Smart, John, 86, 120
Smith, Fairfax, **59**
Smith, Lemuel, 30
Smith, Linus, 59
Snyder, Henry, 112
Sonnastine, B.F., 142
Spencer, 107, **122**
Spencer Township, 8, 11, 13, **28, 103, 112**
Spitzer, C.M., 81
Spooner, Barney, 17
Stearns, Alijah, 144, 147
Stentz and Sheppard, 59
stores, **5-7, 24,** 33, 49, 63, 65, **66**, 91, **119-120, 122- 123, 125-126, 128, 130, 138-140, 153**
Strosecker, Charles, 105
Strosacker, William, 105
Summit County, 8, 20, 120
Sweet, Rowena, 101
Sweitzer barn, 110

Talbot, Edward, 79
temperance/alcohol, 9-10, 45, 50, 67, 99, 101, 119-120, 131
Tiffany, Elijah, 50, 52
Tilley, W.G., 71, 73
tobacco/cigar industry, 9, 31, 109, 116, 124
tools, 7-8, 10, 13, 15, 23, 37-39, 47, 60, 62-63, 93, 109, 119, 137, 141
town halls, **50,** 70, **71, 75**
transportation, 9, 41, 74, 80, 98, 117-118, 124
Tyler, M.D., 101

Underground Railroad/slavery, 9, **24-25, 27,** 50, 52, 98-99
Univeristy of Akron, The/Buchtel College, 5, 99

Valley City/Liverpool Center, **32**, 34, **35-36**, 50, **53, 76,** 91, 102, **105, 124, 128**
Vargo farm, **115**

ventilation, 37, 39, 60-61, 69, 81, 90, 102, 112, 114, 116
Victorian era, 9-11, 47, 57, 60-61, **65**-66, 69, 71, 77, 84, 88, 96, 99-101, 106, 137
voting, 9, 70

Wadsworth, 8-10, 15, 22-23, 30, 41-**42, 46, 50,** 57, 60, 71-**72, 74, 82,** 92, **94,** 109-110, 120, 142
Wadsworth Township, 8, **12,** 15, **17,** 20, **22,** 23, **30,** 41, **43,** 46, 50, 57, **82,** 102, 106, **108-109,** 117, 120
Walcott, Abraham, 40
Wall, John, 82
War of 1812, 7, 10
Warner, E.A., James, 14
Warner, Justus, 8, 119
Warner, Phil, 124
Warner and Webster Company, 112
Washburn, Alva/Lu/Sarah, 101
Webber, Amos, 99
Weed, D.H., 70, 73
Welton, Luther, 119
Welton, Norton, 47
Wertz family, 82
Western Reserve, 7, 10, 23, 26, 29, 32, 36, 38, 51, 70
Western Star, 17, 92
Westfield Center, **89,** 91, **132, 133**
Westfield Township, 8-9, **12, 19, 24, 28, 30, 40, 44, 47,** 69, 91, **111, 116, 129, 132-133**
Weymouth, 23, **38-39,** 41, **45,** 47-**48, 52, 57,** 70, 110, **117,** 119, **122-123, 160**
Whipp, Robert, 99
Whiteside, Alexander, 78, 79
Whiteside, James, 51, 104
Whittesley, 91, 100
Wilder, Austin, 98
Willard, A.M., 71
Wilson, David and John, 10, 75
Wilson's Corners, 10, 91
Windfall, 91
Wolcott, J.W., 40, 79, 122
women, **8,** 11-12, 15, 27, 30, 32, 39, 41, 43, 52, 54-55, 57, **59-60,** 61, **65, 67,** 71, 79, 98-**99, 100,** 101, **106,** 110, 117, 128, 139
wood, 7-8, 10-12, 14, 20, 22- 24, 26, 28, 4, 36, 38, 41, 49, 60-63, 68-70, 76, 80, 87-88, 93, 100, 117-118
Wood, Abel, 26
wool, 9, 119
Wright, Ephraim, 43
Wright, Frank Lloyd, 93

York Township, 8, 15, **22, 33-34,** 35, **54,** 55, **64, 77,** 102, 110, **113-114,** 120-**121**
Young Folk's Gem, 60, 98, 120
Young's Corners, 91